JAVASCRIPT

FOR BEGI

Learn Javascript Language Quickly And Easily With This Comprehensive Guide. Tips and Tricks for Coding and Programming (2022 Crash Course for Newbies)

Edie Clem

TABLE OF CONTENTS

INTRODUCTION

Thanks again for picking this book. There are a lot of books on this subject out there. If you find it useful, please enjoy!

What is JavaScript?

JavaScript is an interpreted programming language, so it is not necessaryto compile the programs to execute them. In other words, programs written with JavaScript can be tested directly in any browser without the need for intermediate processes.

Despite its name, JavaScript has no direct relationship with the Java programming language.

How to include JavaScript in XHTML documents

The integration of JavaScript and XHTML is very flexible since there are at least three ways to include JavaScript code in web pages.

Include JavaScript in the same XHTML document

The JavaScript code is enclosed between <script> tags and is included anywhere in the document. Although it is correct to include any block ofcode in any area of the page, it is recommended to define the JavaScript code within the header of the document (within the <head> tag).

Example of JavaScript code in the document itself </title>

```
<script type = "text / javascript"> alert ("A test
message");

</script>

</head>

<body>

<p> A paragraph of text. </p>

</body>

</html>
```

In order for the resulting XHTML page to be valid, it is necessary to add the type attribute to the < script>. The values included in the type attribute are standardized and in the case of JavaScript, the correct value is text / javascript.

This method is used when defining a small block of code or when you wantto include specific instructions in a specific HTML document that complete the instructions and functions that are included by default in all documents on the website.

The main drawback is that if you want to make a modification to the code block, it is necessary to modify all the pages that include that same block of JavaScript code.

Define JavaScript in an external file

JavaScript instructions can be included in an external JavaScript file that XHTML documents link using the <script> tag. You can create all the necessary JavaScript files and each XHTML document can link as many JavaScript files as you need.

In addition to the type attribute, this method requires defining the src attribute, which indicates the URL corresponding to the JavaScript file to be linked. Each <script> tag can only link a single file, but on the same pageyou can include as many <script> tags as necessary.

JavaScript files are normal text documents with the extension .js, which can be created with any text editor such as Notepad, Wordpad, EmEditor, UltraEdit, Vi, etc.

The main advantage of linking an external JavaScript file is that the XHTML code of the page is simplified, that the same JavaScript code can be reused on all pages of the website and that any modification made to the JavaScript file is immediately reflected in all the XHTML pages that link it.

Include JavaScript in XHTML elements

This last method is the least used, since it consists of including JavaScript pieces within the XHTML code of the page:

<! DOCTYPE html PUBLIC "- // W3C // DTD XHTML 1.0 Transitional // EN" "http://www.w3.org/TR/ xhtml1 / DTD / xhtml1-

transitional.dtd">

```
<html xmlns = "http://www.w3.org/1999/xhtml">

<head>

<meta http -equiv = "Content-Type" content = "text / html; charset = iso-8859-1" />

<title> Example of JavaScript code in the document itself </title>

</head>

<body>

<p onclick = "alert ('A test message')"> A paragraph of text. </p>

</body>

</html>
```

The biggest drawback of this method is that it unnecessarily soils the page's XHTML code and complicates maintenance of the JavaScript code.In general, this method is only used to define some events and in someother special cases, as will be seen later.

Noscript Tag

Some browsers do not have full JavaScript support, other browsers allowyou to partially block it and even some users completely block the use of JavaScript because they believe they are browsing more securely.

7

In these cases, it is common that if the web page requires JavaScript for its correct operation, a warning message to the user is included indicating that you should activate JavaScript to fully enjoy the page. The following example shows a JavaScript-based web page when accessed withJavaScript enabled and when accessed with JavaScript completely disabled.

The following code shows an example of using the <noscript> tag:

<head> ... </head>

<body>

<noscript>

<p> Welcome to My Site </p>

<p> The page you are viewing requires the use of JavaScript for itsoperation.

If you have intentionally disabled it, please enable it again. </p>

</noscript>

/body>

The <noscript> tag must be included inside the <body> tag (usually included at the beginning of <body >). The message that shows <noscript> can include any XHTML element or tag.

Basic Glossary

Script: each of the programs, applications or pieces of code created withthe JavaScript programming language. A few lines of code form a scriptand a file of thousands of lines of JavaScript is also considered a script. Sometimes it is translated into Spanish directly as "escribir", although script is a more appropriate and commonly accepted word.

Sentence: each of the instructions that form a script.

Reserved words: these are the words (in English) that are used to construct JavaScript statements and therefore cannot be used freely.

Syntax

The syntax of a programming language is defined as the set of rules that must be followed when writing the source code of the programs to beconsidered correct for that programming language.

The basic rules that define JavaScript syntax are as follows:

Blank spaces and new lines are not taken into account: as is the case with XHTML, the JavaScript interpreter ignores any remaining blank space, sothe code can be properly sorted to better understand it (tabulating the lines, adding spaces, creating new lines, etc.)

The case is case sensitive: as is the case with the syntax of the XHTMLtags and elements. However, if an XHTML page is used interchangeably,the page is displayed correctly, the only problem being the non-validation of the page. On the other hand, if JavaScript is exchanging upper and lower case letters, the script does not work.

The type of the variables is not defined: when creating a variable, it is not necessary to indicate the type of data that will be stored. In this way, the same variable can store different types of data during script execution.

It is not necessary to end each sentence with the semicolon character (;): in most programming languages, it is mandatory to finish each sentence with the character; Although JavaScript does not require you to do so, it is convenient to follow the tradition of ending each sentence with the semicolon character (;).

Comments can be included: comments are used to add information in the source code of the program. Although the content of the comments is not displayed on the screen, it is necessary to take precautions on the information included in the comments.

JavaScript defines two types of comments: those of a single line and those that occupy several lines.

Example of a single line comment:

// below is an alert message ("test message");

Single line comments are defined by adding two slashes (//) at thebeginning of the line.

Example of multi-line comment:

/ * Multi-line comments are very useful when you

need to include enoughinformation in comments * / alert ("test message");

Multiline comments are defined by enclosing the text of the commentbetween the symbols / * and * /.

Possibilities And Limitations

Since its inception, JavaScript has always been used massively by most Internet sites. The appearance of Flash diminished its popularity since Flash allowed to perform some actions impossible to carry out throughJavaScript.

However, the appearance of AJAX applications programmed with JavaScript has returned an unparalleled popularity within web programming languages.

As for the limitations, JavaScript was designed to run in a very limitedenvironment that would allow users to rely on the execution of the scripts.

In this way, JavaScript scripts cannot communicate with resources that do not belong to the same domain from which the script was downloaded. Nor can scripts close windows that have not opened those same scripts. The windows that are created cannot be too small or too large or placed outside the user's view (although the specific details depend on each browser).

In addition, scripts cannot access the files of the user's computer (neither in read mode nor in write mode) and cannot read or modify browser preferences.

Finally, if the execution of a script lasts too long (for

example due to a programming error), the browser informs the user that a script is consuming too many resources and gives the possibility to stop its execution.

In spite of everything, there are alternatives to be able to skip some of the above limitations. The most used and known alternative is to digitally signthe script and ask the user for permission to perform these actions.

Javascript And Browsers

The most modern browsers currently available include JavaScript supportup to the version corresponding to the third edition of the ECMA-262 standard. The biggest difference lies in the dialect used since while Internet Explorer uses JScript, the rest of browsers (Firefox, Opera, Safari, Konqueror) use JavaScript.

Javascript In Other Environments

The unparalleled popularity of JavaScript as a web application programming language has been extended to other applications and other non-web related environments. Tools like Adobe Acrobat allow you to include JavaScript code in PDF files. Other Adobe tools such as Flash and Flex use ActionScript, a dialect of the same JavaScript standard. Photoshop allows you to make small scripts using JavaScript and Javaversion 6 includes a new package (called javax.script) that allows you to integrate both languages.

CHAPTER 1

WHY JAVASCRIPT?

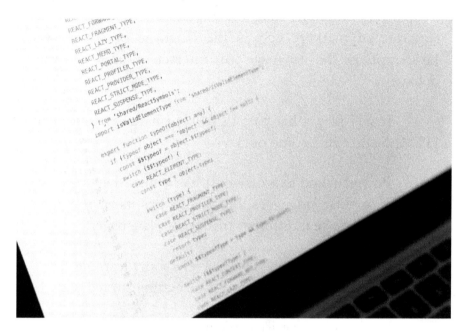

Why Learn Javascript?

Here are a few things to think about:

It is the programming language that web browsers use. All of the most important ones support it and have it turned on by default: Firefox, Chrome, IE, Opera, Safari, and so on. There are other options, but they either need to be installed and activated through plugins or only work in certain browsers.

There is a real fight between browsers to make their

engines run faster and to make JavaScript work better and for your code to run faster. JavaScript, on the other hand, is becoming more stable and faster.

There are no separate HTML and CSS files for it. People play different roles on a web page. HTML is the language of markup, CSS is the language of styles, and JavaScript is the language of interactive and dynamic behavior.

It will play a big part in making it run better when HTML5 and CSS3 come out.

Powerful and expressive: It has syntax that is similar to other popular languages, but it also has its own unique features that make it different from other languages.

Is simple to learn. They have a short learning curve and don't need to spend a lot of time getting started with it.

He is very easy to work with. Do not need a web server or any special software to make things. It is read so we don't have to write code. We don't need to get licenses to do this. This means that you don't need anything else. You just need a text editor (or an editor for code) and a browser. To do this, we can add an add-on like Firebug to help us debug, and we have all the free and free tools we need.

It is the foundation for using AJAX on our pages, which is a programming technique that can be used well to build "new generation" websites that improve the user experience a lot (we will see it in a next post).

The more we learn about JavaScript, the more open

and free frameworks (work environments / libraries) we can use to make our work even easier. These include JQuery, Prototype, Dojo, and more.

It lets us work in an open and standard way without having to follow the rules of any software company. As a bonus, it can work with other popular technologies, like Flash or Java.

JavaScript has been criticized for a lot of the same reasons. It's true that some of these reasons have been used to say that JavaScript is too easy to use. It used to be called "language for amateurs" because it was used to overcrowd visual effects web pages with words. Douglas Crockford's thoughts about it helped people understand it better and make advanced programmers want to learn more about and use it.

Web is a language that makes it easy for people who want to learn how to program to start. In fact, the fact that it's easy to work with has led to it being used as a teaching tool for programming. Like any tool, it has flaws and can be misused. Knowing where its limitations are is one of the first things anyone who wants to start web programming should think about.

Python Vs Javascript: Which One Is Better For Web Development?

It's hard to find someone, a company, or a brand that doesn't have a website right now. Many of these sites are made to be "measured," and in most cases, they do more than the demonstrative and informative ones that corporate sites were made for.

How do you answer these kinds of questions? Even though they are easy to answer, some of us who work in the IT field find them a little upsetting at times. How do you make a new website? What's more? Language: What should I use to make a site look more professional? Python: Is it better for me to learn Python or to learn JavaScript?

When comparing two languages, it's a good idea to point out that they have different syntaxes, but the same paradigms and the same results.

But even though these similarities can be talked about, when it comes to code and web development, they are very different. For this reason, here we'll learn a little about each one, how they work, and which one you should choose.

What is Python?

Python is a minimalist programming language, which contains a syntax that makes it quite simple. It is an interpreted language, that is to say, notcompiled, in addition this serves for all types of development especially to give dynamics to objects in different programs and / or paradigms.

Undoubtedly Python is one of the best options to develop a website, especially when you know the basic elements of language.

Let's see Python what offers us.

Python Features

Before continuing, we will point out some important Python features andwhy you should learn it.

Minimalist Dode

Yes, the code and the simple syntax are perfect for developing websites, facilitating the work and writing of it.

Well Paid

That's right, if you are going to develop a Python website, prepare yourbank account, since the benefit you will receive from developing a Python website will be very profitable, as you can see in Medium.

Multiplatform

Python can not only run it in an operating system, so you can take itanywhere, from free operating systems such as Linux and through thealready known Windows or Mac, in addition to other devices that havesystems based on the aforementioned distributions.

Extensive Libraries

An advantage that comes very well from Python is the amount of librariesor libraries you can find to develop.

There is a wide variety of reusable code, from game creation to largewebsites and quality.

What Is Javascript?

Javascript is a very simple language, which can hardly be interpreted with a browser. This means that it does not need to be compiled for execution.

17

Javascript is highly recommended for the realization ofpages websince it allows the development of the user in it. How? Javascript It allows thewebsite to be as static as possible, and comes hand in hand with other compulsory learning languages, such as HTML and CSS.

What gives interactivity to the web with animations, which allows the userto feel more at ease, since he will not observe a flat website, all this is included in JavaScript.

Normally with JavaScript, programs or applications are created and then inserted into the website to be used. Likewise, they are used to develop mobile applications and complex programs, from the Backend and FrontEnd point of view.

Characteristics of JavaScriptVery Requested

Most of the potential clients ask that their websites be developed in JavaScript, because it is simple and also economical compared to Python.

Easy To Learn

Undoubtedly, this is an advantage that JavaScript has, since it has beenvery well documented in its different stages and has a large community, in which the novice developer can be supported to achieve a learning with solid bases.

Fast And Versatile

Since this is executed with the browser it is very easy

to develop and test improvements, it can also be used to give dynamism and interactivity to a web page and then use that code to create a mobile version of that site.

Good Integration

High level of integration with cloud platforms, such as Amazon Cloud and Heroku. This means that in a large number of cases we have facilities to upload our program with some basic steps unlike Python, which when working with different frameworks requires specific actions that are not always provided by the support, or in any case, not regularly found onplatforms that use Javascript.

Personal Recommendation

Once the characteristics of each language have been analyzed, the most sensible thing to our experience is to immerse yourself in one of them and learn in a staggered way to see if it is to our liking and comfort. It isimportant in programming learning that you have a solid foundation and this is achieved only if you understand the paradigms that make up a language and how to apply these concepts in large-scale projects.

Javascript is an eminently web language. But with Python we can develop many projects of a similar nature, in addition to allowing us to build desktop programs and do additional things, such as scripting or big data.

Once the primary rudiments are known, it is the programmer's duty to delve into things of greater complexity. And although there is contradiction in the subject, the vast majority of people find in learning a framework not only a fast and easy way to create specific programs, but also a lot of learning since knowing a framework allows to delve into programming concepts.

In this sense, the ideal is to start building basic applications or websites to better understand web development and then delve into more complex projects; There are sites like Awwwards where award-winning sites are seen and you can access fresh ideas as well as content that motivates you to continue learning.

There are no strict differences between one language and the other, there is only one gap when the programmer is able to build lines of code in true works of modern art and in binary.

Advantages And Disadvantages Of Javascript

As we have said, JavaScript is a universal language present in numerous HTML pages, in a complementary way to this code. Thanks to JavaScript, HTML pages are more enjoyable and have many additional features.

Knowing how to write scripts in JavaScript means allowing users of your HTML pages to access other functionalities and other services, thereby improving the professionalism of a website. Even recently, when a user first chose a username, it was necessary to click on a button and wait for a response from the server that sometimes asked to restart the procedure since the username already belonged to another person. However today, thanks to the use of AJAX technology, the control is carried out in the background at the same time that the user completes the file. It is undeniable that JavaScript contributes greatly to the ease of use of a website and also increases user loyalty.

Taking into account this important dissemination, knowing how to programin JavaScript has become a basic knowledge for every web developer today.

However, the use of JavaScript is not exclusive to the network; In fact,many programs on the market such as Adobe Photoshop or Adobe Illustrator use versions very similar to JavaScript for automating many tasks.

Tools Conception

Inserted tools that allow JavaScript code are many. There are from the simple text editor such as Windows WordPad to specialized tools such as Aptana Studio, through HTML code editors such as Dreamweaver or FrontPage, which allow you to insert blocks of JavaScript code. The use of these programs allows to have a certain number of tools that facilitate the writing of the code. For example, it is very simple:

Verify a syntax thanks to the automatic coloring of the source code;

Have the function of automatic completion (proposition of available methods or properties of the object);

Know the value of a variable once the script is executed.

Once the design tool is selected, it is convenient to create a programming and test environment to waste as little time as possible in the search for errors that will inevitably arise.

Parameters And Ideal Test Environment

It is necessary to keep in mind that to start working with JavaScript, youneed a minimum of HTML knowledge, especially the notion of tags thatallow you to place yourself on the page. To refresh the memory, we will simply remember that an HTML page is divided into two main parts:

The head where the data corresponding to the description of the contentare located;

The body where the code that makes possible the construction of objectson the page (form fields, text areas, images, etc.) appears.

A JavaScript script can be located, as desired, in one or the other of these two parts. However, in principle, scripts are generally found in the head part of the page. Its execution can be immediate (when the page is loaded) or deferred (click on a button, for example). In this case, it will be necessary to use event-based programming and functions for the code to execute. These points are discussed in the Functions and Events chapter of this book. However, placing the scripts in the head part does not mean that they will be indexed by the search engines. In fact, until now, search enginessuch as Yahoo or Google do not propose any content from these elements of the code, but with the development of Web 2.0 they will do so sooner or later. At the moment, in the case...

HTML And JavaScript

We have previously explained that JavaScript and HTML were closely related, with the HTML code that generally serves as a container for the JavaScript instruction block. Once the HTML page is loaded, the browser executes the JavaScript instructions thus allowing it to be enriched with new features. However, there is another type of JavaScript execution.

The Two Types Of JavaScript Execution

The JavaScript code blocks can be directly present in the source code ofthe HTML page between two tags (one start and one end), or written in a JavaScript file with the extension .js, totally independent of the HTML codeof the page. The first case is known as internal JavaScript as opposed tothe second called external JavaScript.

Neither is better than the other, it is just a programming option. The second option, however, has the advantage of allowing the code to be reused in other HTML pages without the need to rewrite or copy it.

Specifically, the script is written in a special document using a text editor and is saved without formatting under the extension .js. If the editor doesnot propose this extension by default, just add it when saving the document. It is recommended to explicitly name the role that your scriptplays in the HTML page so that it is easier to find it on another occasion.

Once these actions have been carried out, it is very easy to designate the JavaScript file in the HTML page respecting the following syntax:

```
<script src = "javascript_file.js"> </script>
```

Obviously, the file must be present in the same folder on your disk hard or from the server where the corresponding HTML file is located.

The Code Syntax Rules

In view of the fact that JavaScript is a non-flexible language that does not authorize errors, as we can see in the following lines, respecting theserules is essential to start on JavaScript.

1. Upper and lower case

One of the main difficulties of JavaScript is to be a programming language that distinguishes the use of upper and lower case. It is a rule that becomes very important when working with variables and objects.

Specifically, in JavaScript Myobject is not the same as myobject.

This applies to all keywords (properties, methods, JavaScript functions)and the use of design tools such as Aptana or the Dreamweaver editor facilitates the identification of this syntax since they are almost instantly identified with colors.

Another syntactic rule refers to the insertion of comments.

2. Inserting comments

As in most programming languages, inserting comments into your scriptscan be extremely useful. In fact, apart from being able to more easily find the instruction blocks that you have created, the comments can be of immense help the day you have to retake the code. The readability of the code is even one of the main criteria determining the quality of a JavaScript code. Because, after all, how about...

Creating The Test Page

To write effectively in the HTML pages, it is best to create a model page where you must include the labels that indicate the beginning and end ofthe script .

Being the head part of the page where the JavaScript code is usuallyinserted, look at this example of the HTML code of the model page that will be used for writing all your scripts.

The first two lines determine the type of document, its presence is essential for the proper functioning of DHTML instructions, as we will see in thechapter Improve interactivity with JavaScript and CSS. The fourth line indicates the beginning of the head tag that interests us in a particular way. The fifth line allows you to add a meta tag that indicates the charactersused, the sixth gives a title to the page (in our case, JavaScript ModelPage).

Creating A Personal Library Of Javascript Scripts

Over time, you will have to develop numerous scripts that can be reused later. To facilitate this reuse, identify your pages with names that clearly ndicate the purpose of your JavaScript script.

25

Beware of confusing personal library scripts and common libraries,abundant in the network, and that enrich the classic JavaScript operation. The installation of new JavaScript libraries will be discussed in the chapter Improving interactivity with JavaScript and CSS.

Error Messages And Tips For Debugging The Code (Debug)

The fact that browsers interpret JavaScript differently, imposes the need to perform tests on each of them. However, the best advice is to test thescripts first in Firefox / Mozilla which has a more powerful error resolutiontool and then perform a test in Internet Explorer. To help you a little in processing possible errors; we can divide these into different categories:

First, it may be the case that nothing happens loading the page. It is necessary to know that JavaScript controls the script before displaying anything. If it finds an error, the script is interrupted without going too far. These errors are usually due to approximate syntax or keyboard errors.

It is also possible to find errors not when loading the page but when it is executed. This generally means that objects, their properties, their methods and even functions do not correspond or are misused.

Finally, the most difficult errors to detect are the purely logical errors that arise when the script tests have not been sufficient. In these cases, thescript can work in one case and cause an error with other values or other circumstances. Do not hesitate to test your scripts with different values and carefully observe the results obtained.

By prudence, if you do not have atool that allows you to control the state of the script (such as Aptana ...

JavaScript Debugging Tools

Although it is possible to write a script in a very simple way, the use of a design tool It can be useful, especially if it is the resolution of an error. Itsuse will allow us to have breakpoints, know the value of the variables and other aids that will be very useful in this crucial stage such as the search for an error.

We are going to introduce some of these tools:

1. Microsoft Script Debugger

With the use of Microsoft Script Debugger, you have a tool to help with syntax and problem solving, when the Internet Explorer browser encounters a problem in the development of a script, in Microsoft Script Debugger it is possible to go directly to the line that presents the problem.

2. Microsoft FrontPage / Adobe Dreamweaver

The HTML code editors allow you to view the code of the page and thus access the JavaScript part. But they do not have functionalities capable of adding breakpoints and knowing the value of the variables.

CHAPTER 2

BASIC PROGRAMMING

Before you start making programs and utilities with JavaScript, you need to know what the basic parts of the applications are. In this chapter, if you already know how to write code in another programming language, you will learn how to write JavaScript code.

If you've never programmed before, this chapter will teach you everything you need to know in order to understand more advanced programming, which is used to make real apps.

Variables

The variables in the programming languages follow a logic similar to the variables used in other fields such as mathematics. A variable is an element that is used to store and reference another value. Thanks to the variables it is possible to create "generic programs", that is, programs that always work the same regardless of the specific values used.

In the same way that if in Mathematics the variables did not exist theequations and formulas could not be defined, in programming one couldnot make really useful programs without the variables. If there were no variables, a program that adds two numbers could be written as: result = 3

+ 1

The previous program is so unhelpful that it only applies to the case where the first number of the sum is 3 and the second number is 1. In any other case, the program obtains an incorrect result.

However, the program can be remade as follows using variables to storeand refer to each number:

n

umber_

1 = 3

number

_2 = 1

result =

number

_1   +

number

_2

Elements number_1 and number_2 are variables that store the values used by the program. The result is always calculated based on the value storedby the variables, so this program works correctly for any number of indicated numbers. If the value of the variables number_1 and number_2 is modified, the program continues to function correctly.

Variables in JavaScript are created using the reserved word var. In thisway, the previous example can be done in JavaScript as follows:

```
        var
number_1  =  3;
var number_2 =
1; var  result  =
number_1     +
number_2;
```

The reserved word var should only be indicated when defining the variable for the first time, which is called declaring a variable. When the variablesare used in the rest of the script instructions, it is only necessary to indicate their name. In other words, in the previous example it would be a mistaketo indicate the following:

var number_1 = 3; var number_2 = 1;

var result = var number_1 + var number_2;

If a value is also assigned when a variable is declared, it is said that the variable has been initialized. In JavaScript, it is not mandatory to initializethe variables since they can be declared by one party and assign them a value later. Therefore, the previous example can be remade as follows:

var number_1; var number_2;

number_1 = 3; number_2 = 1; var result = number_1 + number_2;

One of the most surprising features of JavaScript for programmers accustomed to other programming languages is that it is not necessary to declare the variables. In other words, you can use variables that have not been previously defined by the reserved word var. The previous example is also correct in JavaScript as follows:

var

number_1 = 3;

var   number_2

= 1;   result =

number_1   +

number_2;

The result variable is not declared, so JavaScript

creates a global variable (the differences between local and global variables will be seen later) and assigns it the corresponding value. In the same way, the following code would also be correct:

```
n
umber_1
=    3;
number_
2  =  1;
result  =
number_
1    +
number_
2;
```

In any case, it is recommended to declare all the variables to be used.

The name of a variable is also known as an identifier and must comply withthe following rules:

' It can only consist of letters, numbers, and the symbols $ (dollar) and _(underscore).
' The first character cannot be a number.

Therefore, the following variables have correct names:

var $ number1; var _ $ letter; var $$$

otherNumber; var $ _ to $ 4;However, the following variables have incorrect identifiers:

var 1number;// Start with a number var number; 1_123; // Contains acharacter ";"

Types Of Variables

Although all JavaScript variables are created in the same way (using the reserved word var), the way in which they are assigned a value depends on the type of value to be stored (numbers, texts, etc.)

Numeric

They areused to store integer numerical values (called integer in English) or decimals (called float in English). In this case, the value is assigned by directly indicating the integer or decimal number. Decimal numbers use the character. (period) instead of, (comma) to separate the whole part and the decimal part:

var iva = 16 // integer variable var total = 234.65; // decimal type variable

Text Strings

Used to store characters, words and/or text phrases. To assign the value to the variable, the value is enclosed in double or single quotes, to delimit its beginning and its end:

var message = "Welcome to our website"; var productName = 'ProductABC'; var Selected letter = 'c';

Sometimes, the text that is stored in the variables is not so simple. If, for example, the text itself contains single or double quotes, the strategy followed is to enclose the text with quotes (single or double) that the text does not use:

/ * The content of text1 has single quotes, so it is enclosed with double quotes * /

var text1 = "A phrase with 'single quotes' inside";

/ * The content of text2 has double quotes, so it is enclosed with single quotes * /

var text2 = 'A phrase with "double quotes" inside';

However, sometimes text strings contain both single and double-quotes. In addition, there are other characters that are difficult to include in a text variable (tab, ENTER, etc.). To solve these problems, JavaScript defines a mechanism to easily include special and problematic characters within atext string.

The mechanism consists of replacing the problematic character with a simple combination of characters. In this way, the previous example that contained single and double quotes within the text can be redone as follows:

var text1 = 'A phrase with \' single quotes \ 'inside'; var text2 = "A phrasewith \" double quotes \ "inside";

Arrays

Sometimes, arrays are called vectors, matrices, and even arrays. However, the term array is the most used and is a commonly accepted word in the programming environment.

An array is a collection of variables, which can be all of the same type or each of a different type. Its utility is better understood with a simple example: if an application needs to handle the days of the week, seven variables of type text could be created:

var day1 = "Monday"; var day2 = "Tuesday"; ... var day7 = "Sunday";

Although the previous code is not incorrect, it is inefficient and complicates the programming excessively. If instead of the days of the week you had to save the name of the months of the year, the name of all the countries in the world or the daily temperature measurements of the last 100 years, you would have to create tens or hundreds of variables.

In these types of cases, all related variables can be grouped into a collection of variables or array. The previous example can be remade as follows: var days = ["Monday", "Tuesday", "Wednesday", "Thursday", "Friday", "Saturday", "Sunday"];

Now, a single variable called days stores all related values, in this case, the days of the week. To define an array, the characters [and] are used todelimit its beginning and end and the character, (comma) is used to separate its elements: var array_name = [value1, value2, ..., valueN];

Once an array is defined, it is very easy to access each of its elements.Each element is accessed indicating its position within the array. The only complication, which is responsible for many errors when starting to program, is that the positions of the elements begin to be counted at 0 and not at 1:

var day Selected = days [0]; // selected day = "Monday" var otherDay =days [5]; // otherDay = "Saturday"

In the previous example, the first instruction wants to get the first elementof the array. To do this, the name of the array is indicated and in square brackets the position of the element within the array. As mentioned, the positions begin to be counted at 0, so the first element occupies the position 0 and is accessed through days [0].

The days value [5] refers to the element that occupies the sixth position within the days array. As the positions begin to be counted at 0, position 5 refers to the sixth element, in this case, the Saturday value.

Booleans

Booleans or Boolean type variables are also known as logical type variables. Although to really understand its usefulness you should study the advanced programming with JavaScript in the following chapter, its basic operation is very simple.

A variable of type boolean stores a special type of value that can only take two values: true (true) or false (false). It cannot be used to store numbers, nor can it save text strings.

The only values that can store these variables are true and false, so thetrue and false values cannot be used. Below are a couple of Booleanvariables:

var Registered client = false; var vatIncluded = true;

Operators

Variables alone are of little use. Until now, we have only seen how to create variables of different types and how to show their value through the alert () function. To make really useful programs, other tools are necessary.

Operators allow you to manipulate the value of variables, performmathematical operations with their values and compare different variables.In this way, operators allow programs to perform complex calculations and make logical decisions based on comparisons and other types of conditions.

Assignment

The assignment operator is the most used and the easiest. This operator is used to store a specific value in a variable. The symbol used is = (not to be confused with the operator == that will be seen later): var number1 = 3;

To the left of the operator, the name of a variable must always be indicated. To the right of the operator, you can indicate variables, values, logicalconditions, etc:

var number1 = 3; var number2 = 4;

/ * Error, the assignment is always made to a variable, so on the left, you cannot indicate a number * /

5 = number1;

// Now, variable number1 is worth 5 number1 = 5;

// Now, the variable number1 is worth 4 number1 = number2;

Increase And Decrease

These two operators are only valid for numerical variables and are used toincrease or decrease the variable value by one unit.

Example:

va

r number

= 5; ++

number;

alert

(number

); //

number

= 6

The increment operator is indicated by the prefix ++ in the variable name. The result is that the value of that variable is increased by one unit. Therefore, the previous example is equivalent to:

var number = 5; number = number + 1; alert (number);

// number = 6

Equivalently, the decrement operator (indicated as a prefix - in the name ofthe variable) is used to decrease the value of the variable:

```
var number = 5; --number; alert (number); // number = 4
```

The previous example is equivalent to:

var number = 5; number = number - 1; alert (number);
// number = 4

The increment and decrement operators can not only be indicated as aprefix of the variable name, but it is also possible to use them as a suffix. In this case, their behavior is similar but very different. In the following example:

```
var number = 5;
number++;
alert(number); // number = 6
```

The result of executing the previous script is the same as when the ++ number operator is used, so it may seem equivalent to indicate the ++ operator in front of or behind the variable identifier. However, the following example shows their differences:

```
var number1 = 5; var number2 = 2; number3 =
```

number1 ++ + number2; // number3 = 7, number1 = 6

var number1 = 5; var number2 = 2; number3 = ++ number1 + number2;

// number3 = 8, number1 = 6

If the ++ operator is indicated as a prefix of the variable identifier, its valueis increased before performing any other operation. If the ++ operator is indicated as a variable identifier suffix, its value is increased after executing the statement in which it appears.

Therefore, in the instruction number3 = number1 ++ + number2 ;, the value of number1 is increased after the operation (first it is added and number3 is worth 7, then the value of number1 is increased and is worth 6). However,in the instruction number3 = ++ number1 + number2 ;, first the value of number1 is increased and then the sum is made (first it increases number1 and voucher 6, then the sum is made and number3 voucher 8).

Logical

Logical operators are essential for complex applications, as they are usedto make decisions about the instructions that the program should execute based on certain conditions.

The result of any operation that uses logical operators is always a logical or Boolean value.

Denial

One of the most used logical operators is that of

negation. It is used toobtain the opposite value of the variable:

> var visible = true;

> alert (! visible); // Show "false" and not "true"

Logical denial is obtained by presetting the symbol! to the variable identifier. If the original variable is of Boolean type, it is very simple toobtain its negation. However, what happens when the variable is a numberor a text string? To obtain the negation in this type of variables, it is first carried out its conversion to a Boolean value:

' If the variable contains a number, it becomes false if it is 0 and true forany other number (positive or negative, decimal or whole).

' If the variable contains a text string, it becomes false if the string is empty ("") and true in any other case.

> var quantity = 0; empty =! quantity; // empty = true

> quantity = 2; empty =! quantity; // empty = false
> var message = ""; emptymessage =! message; // empty=
> true message; message = "Welcome";

> empty message =! message; // Empty message = false

AND

The logical AND operation obtains its result by combining two Booleanvalues. The operator is indicated by the && symbol and its result is onlytrue if the operands hold true.

42

OR

The logical OR operation also combines two Boolean values. The operatoris indicated by the symbol || and its result is true if either of the two operands is true.

Mathematics

JavaScript allows you to perform mathematical manipulations on the valueof numerical variables. The operators defined are: addition (+), subtraction (-), multiplication (*) and division (/). Example:

var number1 = 10; var number2 = 5;

result = number1 / number2; // result = 2 result = 3 + number1;   //
result = 13 result = number 2-4;   //
result = 1 result = number1 *number 2; // result = 50

In addition to the four basic operators, JavaScript defines anothermathematical operator that is not easy to understand when it is first studied, but which is very useful on some occasions.

This is the "module" operator, which calculates the rest of the entire division of two numbers. If you divide 10 and 5 for example, the division is exactand gives a result of 2. The rest of that division is 0, so module 10 and 5 equals 0.

However, if you divide 9 and 5, the division is not exact, the result is 1 and the remainder 4, so module 9 and 5 equals 4.

The JavaScript module operator is indicated by the% symbol, which should not be confused with the percentage calculation :

var number1 = 10; var number2 = 5; result = number1% number2; // result

= 0

number1 = 9; number2 = 5;

result = number1% number2; // result = 4

Mathematical operators can also be combined with the assignmentoperator to abbreviate their notation:

var number1 = 5; number1 + = 3; // number1 = number1 + 3 = 8 number1 -

= 1; // number1 = number1 - 1 = 4 number1 * =
2;   // number1 =number1 * 2 =
10 number1 / = 5;   // number1 = number1 / 5
= 1number1% = 4;   // number1 = number1% 4 =
1

Relational

The relational operators defined by JavaScript are identical to those that define mathematics.

Operators that relate variables are essential for any complex application, as will be seen in the next chapter on advanced programming. The result of all these operators is always a Boolean value.

Special care must be taken with the equality operator (==), as it is thesource of most programming errors, even for users who already have some experience developing scripts. The == operator is used to compare thevalue of two variables, so it is very different from the = operator, which is used to assign a value to a variable:

// The operator "=" assigns values var number1 = 5; result = number1 = 3;

// number1 = 3 and result = 3

// The operator "==" compares variables var number1 = 5; result = number1 == 3; // number1 = 5 and result = false

Relational operators can also be used with variables of type text string:var text1 = "hello"; var text2 = "hello"; var text3 = "goodbye";

result = text1 == text3; // result = false result = text1! = text2; // result = false result = text3> = text2; // result = false

When text strings are used, the operators "greater than" (>) and "less than" (<) follow a non-intuitive reasoning: letter by letter is compared starting from the left until a difference is found Between the two text strings. To determine if one letter is greater or less than another, uppercase letters are considered lower than lower case letters and the first letters of the alphabet are smaller than the last ones (a is less than b, b is less than c, A is lessthan a, etc.)

Flow Control Structures

Programs that can be performed using only variables and operators are a simple linear sequence of basic instructions.

However, programs that show a message cannot be carried out if the value of a variable is equal to a certain value and does not show the message inall other cases. Nor can the same instruction be repeated efficiently, suchas adding a certain value to all the elements of an array.

To carry out this type of programs, flow control structures are necessary, which are instructions of the type "if this condition is met, do it; if it is notmet, do this another". There are also instructions such as "repeat this while this condition is met".

If flow control structures are used, the programs cease to be a linear sequence of instructions to become intelligent programs that can makedecisions based on the value of the variables.

If Structure

The structure most used in JavaScript and in most programming languages is the if structure. It is used to make decisions based on a condition. Its formal definition is:

```
if (condition) {...

}
```

If the condition is met (that is, if its value is true), all instructions within {...} are executed. If the condition is not met (that is if its value is false), no instruction contained in {...} is executed and the program continues executing the rest of the instructions in the script.

Exam

ple: var show

Message   =

true; if (show

Message) {

    alert ("Hello World");

    }

Here the message is shown to the user since the variable ShowMessagehas a value of true and therefore, the program enters into the if instruction block.

The example could also be rewritten as:
var show Message = true; if (show Message == true) { alert ("Hello World");
    }

In this case, the condition is a comparison between the value of the variable Show message and the value true. As the two values coincide, the equality is met and therefore the condition is true, its value is true and the instructions contained in that if block are executed.

The comparison of the previous example is usually

the origin of manyprogramming errors, by confusing the == and = operators. Comparisonsare always made with the operator == since the operator = only assigns values: var show Message = true;

// The two if values are compared (show Message == false) {...

}

// Error - The value "false" is assigned to the variable if (show Message =false) {...

}

The condition that controls the if () you can combine the different logicaland relational operators shown above:

```
var shown = false; if (! shown) {
    alert ("This is the first time the message is displayed");
}
```

The AND and OR operators allow you to chain several simple conditions tobuild complex conditions:

```
var shown = false; var
user PermitMessages = true;if (!
displayed && user Allow
Messages) {

    alert ("This is the first time the message is displayed");
}
```

The previous condition is formed by an AND operation on two variables. In turn, the negation operator is applied to the first variable before performing the AND operation. Thus, since the value of displayed is false, the value! Displayed would be true. Since the variable UserPermitMessages is true,the result of! Displayed && userPermitMessages would be equal to true && true, so the final result of the condition of the if () would be true and therefore, the instructions inside the block are executed of if (). Exercise 5

Complete the conditions of the if in the following script so that the messages of the alerts () are always displayed correctly:

```
var
number1    =
5;          var
number2    =
8;if (...) {

    alert ("number1 is not greater than number2");

    } if (...) {

    alert ("number2 is positive");

    } if (...) {

    alert ("number1 is negative or nonzero");

    } if (...) {alert ("Increasing the value ofby 1 unit
```

does not make it greater than or equal to number1number2");

}

Structure if ... else

Sometimes, the decisions to be made are not of the type "if the condition is met, do it; if it is not met, do nothing." Normally the conditions are usually of the type "if this condition is met, do it; if it is not met, do this another".

For this second type of decision, there is a variant of the if structure called if

... else. Its formal definition is as follows:

if (condition) {...

} else {...

}

If the condition is met (that is if its value is true), all the instructions found within the if () are executed. If the condition is not met (that is, if its value is false), all instructions contained in else {} are executed. Example:

```
var age = 18; if (age> = 18) {
    alert ("You are of legal age");

    } else {

    alert ("You are still a minor");

    }
```

If the value of the variable age is greater than or equal to the numericalvalue 18, the condition of the if () is fulfilled and therefore, its instructionsare executed and the message "You are of age" is displayed. However, when the value of the age variable is not equal to or greater than 18, the condition of the if () is not met, so all the instructions in the else {} block are automatically executed. In this case, the message "You are still a minor" would be displayed.

The following example compares variables of type text string:var name = "";

```
if (name == "") {

alert ("You haven't told us your name yet");

} else {

alert ("We have saved your name");

}
```

The condition of the previous if () is constructed using the == operator,which is used to compare two values (not to be confused with the operator

= used to assign values). In the previous example, if the text string stored in the variable name is empty (that is, it is equal to ""), the message defined in the if () is displayed. Otherwise, the message defined in the else {} block is displayed.

The if ... else structure can be chained to perform several checks in a row:if (age <12) {

alert ("You are still too small");

} else if (age <19) {

alert ("You are a teenager");

} else if (age <35) {

alert ("You are still young");

} else {

alert ("Think about taking care of yourself a little more"); }

It is not mandatory that the combination of structures if ... else ends withthe else statement, since it can end with an else type instruction if ().

Structure for

The structures if and if ... else are not very efficient when you want to repeatedly execute an instruction. For example, if you want to display a message five times, you might think about using the following if:

var times = 0; if (times <4) {
        alert ("Message"); times ++;

}

It is checked if the variable times is less than 4. If it

is fulfilled, it enters the if(), the message is displayed and the value of the variable is increased times. This should continue to run until the message is displayed five times as desired.

However, the actual operation of the previous script is very different from the desired one, since the message is only shown once per screen. The reason is that the execution of the if () structure is not repeated and the condition check is only done once, regardless of whether the value of the variable used in the condition is modified within the if ().

The for structure allows you to perform this type of repetitions (also called loops) in a very simple way. However, its formal definition is not as simple as that of if ():

for (initialization; condition; update) {...

}

The idea of the operation of a for loop is as follows: "as long as the indicated condition is still fulfilled, repeats the execution of the instructions defined within the for. In addition, after each repetition, it updates the value of the variables used in the condition ".

' "Initialization" is the area in which the initial values of the variables that control the repetition are established.

' The "condition" is the only element that decides whether the repetition continues or stops.

' The "update" is the new value that is assigned after

each repetition to thevariables that control the repetition.

```
var
message    =
"Hi, I'm in a
loop";    for
(var i = 0; i
<5; i ++) {

    alert (message);

}
```

The part of the loop initialization consists of:

```
var i = 0;
```

Therefore, the variable i is created first and assigned the value of 0. This initialization zone is only taken into account just before starting to executethe loop.

The following repetitions do not take into account this initialization part.

The condition zone of the loop is:

```
i <5
```

The loops continue to run as long as the conditions are met and stop executing just after verifying that the condition is not met. In this case, while the variable i is worth less than 5 the loop is executed indefinitely.

Since the variable i has been initialized to a value of 0 and the condition to exit the loop is that i is less than 5, if the value of i is not modified in anyway, the loop would be repeated indefinitely.

For this reason, it is essential to indicate the update zone, in which thevalue of the variables that control the loop is modified: i ++

In this case, the value of the variable i is increased by one unit after each repetition. The update zone is executed after the execution of the instructions included in the for.

Thus, during the execution of the fifth repetition the value of i will be 4. After the fifth execution, the value of i is updated, which will now be worth 5.Since the condition is that i is less than 5, the condition is no longer complies and for instructions are not executed a sixth time.

Normally, the variable that controls the loops for is called i, since it remembers the word index and its short name saves a lot of time andspace.

The previous example that showed the days of the week contained in an array can be redone more easily using the structure for:

var days = ["Monday", "Tuesday", "Wednesday", "Thursday", "Friday", "Saturday Sunday"];

for (var i = 0; i <7; i ++) { alert (days [i]);
    }

Structure for ... in

A control structure derived from for is the structure for ... in. Its exactdefinition implies the use of objects, which is an advanced programming element that is not going to be studied. Therefore, only the for ... in structure adapted to its use in arrays will be presented. Its formal definition adapted to arrays is:

```
for (index in array) {...

}
```

If you want to traverse all the elements that form an array, the structure for

... in is the most efficient way to do it, as shown in the following example:

```
var days = ["Monday", "Tuesday", "Wednesday", "Thursday", "Friday","Saturday", "Sunday"];

for (i in days) { alert (days [i]);

}
```

The variable indicated as an index is the one that can be used within the for

... in loop to access the array elements. In this way, in the first repetition of the loop the variable i is worth 0 and in the last voucher 6.

This control structure is the most suitable for traversing arrays (and objects) since it avoids having to indicate the initialization and conditions of the loop for simple and works correctly whatever the length of the array. In fact, itstill works the same even if the number of array elements varies.

Functions And Basic Properties Of Javascript

JavaScript incorporates a series of tools and utilities (called functions and properties, as will be seen later) for handling variables. In this way, many of the basic operations with the variables can be performed directly with the utilities offered by JavaScript.

Useful functions for text strings

Below are some of the most useful functions for handling text strings:

length, calculates the length of a text string (the number of characters thatmake it up)

var message = "Hello World" ;

var numberLetters = message.length; // numberLetters = 10

+, is used to concatenate several text strings

var message1 = "Hello"; var message2 = "World";

var message = message1 + message2; // message = "Hello World"In addition to the + operator, you can also use the concat () function

var message1 = "Hello";

var message2 = message1.concat ("World"); //

message2 = "Hello World"Text strings can also be joined with numerical variables:

var variable1 = "Hello"; var variable2 = 3;

var message = variable1 + variable2; // message = "Hello 3"

When several text strings are joined, it is usual to forget to add a spacebetween the words:

var message1 = "Hello"; var message2 = "World";

var message = message1 + message2; // message = "HelloWorld"

Blank spaces can be added at the end or beginning of the strings and canalso be explicitly indicated:

var message1 = "Hello"; var message2 = "World";

var message = message1 + "" + message2; // message = "Hello World"

toUpperCase (), transforms all the characters in the string to their corresponding characters in uppercase:

var message1 = "Hello";

var message2 = message1.toUpperCase (); // message2 = "HELLO"

toLowerCase (), transforms

58

all the characters in the string to their corresponding characters in lowercase:

var message1 = "HolA";

var message2 = message1.toLowerCase (); // message2 = "hello"charAt (position), get the character that is in the indicated position:

var message = "Hello"; var letter = message.charAt (0); // letter = H letter = message.charAt (2);// letter = l

indexOf (character), calculates the position where the indicated character is within the text string. If the character is included several times within thetext string, its first position is returned starting to search from the left. If the string does not contain the character, the function returns the value -1:

var message = "Hello"; var position = message.indexOf ('a'); // position = 3 position = message.indexOf ('b'); // position = -1 Its analogous function is lastIndexOf ():

lastIndexOf (character), calculates the last position in which the indicated character is within the text string. If the string does not contain the character, the function returns the value -1:

var message = "Hello"; var position = message.lastIndexOf ('a'); // position

= 3 position = message.lastIndexOf ('b'); // position = -1

The lastIndexOf () function starts its search from the end of the string to the beginning, although the position returned is correct starting from the beginning of the word. substring (start, end), extracts a portion of a text string. The second parameter is optional. If only the start parameter is indicated, the function returns the part of the corresponding original string from that position to the end:

var message = "Hello World"; var portion = message.substring (2); // portion = "the World" portion = message.substring (5); // portion = "World" portion = message.substring (7);   // portion = "ndo"

If a negative start is indicated, the same original string is returned: var message = "Hello World";

var portion = message.substring (-2); // portion = "Hello World"

When the beginning and end are indicated, the part of the original chain between the initial position and the one immediately preceding the final position is returned (that is, the start position is included and the positionfinal no):

var message = "Hello World"; var portion = message.substring (1, 8); // portion = "wave Mun" portion = message.substring (3, 4);

// portion

= "a"

If an ending smaller than the beginning is indicated, JavaScript considers them in reverse, since it automatically assigns the smallest value at the beginning and the largest at the end:

var message = "Hello World"; var portion = message.substring (5, 0); // portion = "Hello" portion = message.substring (0, 5);

// portion ="Hello"

split (separator), convert a text string into an array of text strings. Thefunction starts the text string by determining its chunks from the indicated separator character:

var message = "Hello World, I am a text string!"; var words = message.split("");

// words = ["Hello", "World,", "I am", "a", "string", "of", "text!"]; With thisfunction you can easily extract the letters that form a word:

var word = "Hello"; var letters = word.split (""); // letters = ["H", "o", "l", "a"]

Useful functions for numbers

Below are some of the most useful functions and

properties for handlingnumbers.

NaN, (from English, "Not a Number") JavaScript uses the NaN value toindicate an undefined numerical value (for example, division 0/0).

var number1 = 0; var number2 = 0;

alert (number1 / number2); // the value NaN

isNaN () is shown, it allows to protect the application from possibleundefined numerical values

var number1 = 0; var number2 = 0; if (isNaN (number1 / number2)) {alert ("The division is not defined for the indicated numbers");

} else {

alert ("The division is equal to =>" + number1 / number2); }

Infinity, refers to an infinite and positive numerical value (there is also the −Infinity value for negative infinities)

var number1 = 10; var number2 = 0;

alert (number1 / number2); // the Infinityvalue is displayed

toFixed (digits), returns the original number with as many decimals as indicated by the digits parameter and performs the necessary rounding. It isa very useful function for example to show prices.

```
var number1 = 4564.34567; number1.toFixed (2); // 4564.35 issue1.toFixed
```

```
(6); // 4564.345670 issue1.toFixed (); // 4564
```

CHAPTER 3

ADVANCED PROGRAMMING

It's easy to write simple or medium-sized scripts with the control structures, operators, and other JavaScript tools that we've seen in the past chapters.

However, for more complex applications, things like functions and other more advanced control structures are needed. This chapter talks about these things more in depth.

Functions

When developing a complex application, it is very common to use the same instructions over and over again.

A script for an e-commerce store, forexample, has to calculate the total price of the products several times, to add taxes and shipping costs.

When a series of instructions are repeated over and over again, the source code of the application becomes too complicated, since:

' The application code is much longer because many instructions are repeated.

' If you want to modify any of the repeated instructions, you should makeas many modifications as you have written that instruction, which becomes very heavy work and very prone to mistakes.

Functions are the solution to all these problems, both in JavaScript and in other programming languages. A function is a set of instructions that are grouped together to perform a specific task and that can be easily reused.

In the following example, the instructions that add the two numbers andshow a message with the result are repeated over and over again:

var result;

var number1 = 3; var number2 = 5;

// The numbers are added and the result result is shown = number1 +number2; alert ("The result is" + result);

number1 = 10; number2 = 7;

// The numbers are added and the result result is shown = number1 +number2; alert ("The result is" + result);

number1 = 5; number2 = 8;

// The numbers are added and the resultis shown

result= number1 + number2; alert ("The result is" + result); ...

Although it is a very simple example, it seems clear that repeating thesame instructions throughout the code is not recommended. The solution proposed by the functions consists in extracting the instructions that are repeated and replacing them with an instruction of the type "at this point,the instructions that have been extracted are executed":

var result;

var number1 = 3; var number2 = 5;

/ * At this point, the function that adds

2 numbers is called

and shows the result * /
number1 = 10; number2 = 7;

/ * At this point, the function that adds

2 numbers is called

and displays the result * /

number1 = 5; number2 = 8;

/ * At this point, the function that adds

2 numbers is called and shows the result * / ...

For the solution of the previous example to be valid, the common instructions must be grouped into a function that can be Indicate the numbers to add before displaying the message.

Therefore, you must first create the basic function with the common instructions. Functions in JavaScript are defined by the reserved word function, followed by the name of the function. Its formal definition is as follows:

function function_name () {...

}

The function name is used to call that function when necessary. Theconcept is the same as with the variables, which are assigned a unique name to be able to use them within the code. After the name of the function, two parentheses are included whose meaning is detailed below. Finally, the symbols {and} are used to enclose all the instructions that belong to the function (similar to how the instructions are enclosed in the ifor for structures).

Returning to the previous example, a function called sum_and_sample is created as follows:

function   sum_and_sample () { result =

number1 + number2; alert ("The result is" + result); }

Although the previous function is created correctly, it does not work as it should because the "arguments" are missing, which are explained in thenext section. Once the function has been created, the function can becalled from any point in the code to execute its instructions

(in addition to "calling the function", the expression "invoke the function" is also used).

The function call is made simply by indicating its name, including the end brackets and the character; to finish the instruction:

```
function sum_and_sample () {
```

result = number1 + number2; alert ("The result is" + result);

```
} var result;
```

```
var number1 = 3; var number2
= 5; sum_and_sample ();number1 =
10; number2 = 7; sum_and_sample ();
number1 = 5; number2 = 8;
```

```
sum_and_sample (); ...
```

The code in the previous example is much more efficient than the first code that was shown since there are no repeated instructions. The instructions that add and display messages have been grouped under one function, which allows them to be executed at any point in the program simply by indicating the name of the function.

The only thing missing from the previous example to function correctly is to be able to indicate to the function the numbers to add. When data needs to be passed to a function, the "arguments" are used, as explained in the next section.

Arguments And Return Values

The simplest functions do not need any information to produce their results. However, most functions of real applications must access the value of some variables to produce their results.

The variables that functions need are called arguments. Before you canuse them, the function must indicate how many arguments you need and what is the name of each argument. In addition, when invoking the function, the values that will be passed to the function must be included. The arguments are indicated within the parentheses that go after the name ofthe function and are separated by a comma (,).

Following the previous example, the function must indicate that it needstwo arguments, corresponding to the two numbers that it has to add: function sum_and_sample (firstNumber, secondNumber) {...}

Next, to use the value of the arguments within the function, the same name with which the arguments were defined should be used:

```
function          sum_and_sample          (firstNumber,
secondNumber) {...}
```

```
var result = firstNumber + secondNumber; alert ("The
result is" + result); }
```

Within the function, the value of the variable
firstNumber will be equal to the first value that is passed to
the function and the value of the variablesecondNumber will
be equal to the second value that is passed to it. Topass
values to the function, they are included in the
parentheses usedwhen calling the function: Function

```
//definition          function          sum_and_sample
(firstNumber,  secondNumber)  {...}  var  result  =
firstNumber + secondNumber; alert ("The result is" +
result);
```

```
}
```

```
// Declaration of the variables var number1 = 3; var
number2 = 5;
```

```
//    Call   to   the   function
sum_and_sample (number1, number2);In
```
the previous code, it should be taken into
account that:

'   Although variables are almost always used to pass the
data to the function, the value of these variables could have
been used directly: sum_and_sample (3, 5);

' The number of arguments passed to a function should be the same as the number of arguments indicated by the function. However, JavaScript does not show any errors if more or less arguments are passed than necessary.

' The order of the arguments is fundamental since the first data indicated in the call will be the first value expected by the function; The second value indicated in the call is the second value that the function expects and so on.

' An unlimited number of arguments can be used, although if their numberis very large, the function call is complicated too much.

' It is not mandatory to match the name of the arguments used by the function and the name of the arguments. Previously, the arguments passed are number1 and number2 and the arguments used by the function are firstNumber and secondNumber.

Below is another example of a function that calculates the total price of aproduct from its basic price:

// Function definition function calculates Total Price (price) {

var taxes = 1.16; var expenses Shipping = 10; var Total price = (price *taxes) + expenses Shipping;

}

// Call to the function calculates Total Price (23.34);

The previous function takes as an argument a variable called price andadds taxes and shipping costs to obtain the total price. When calling the function, the value of the basic price is passed directly by number 23.34.

However, the previous code is not too useful, since the ideal would be that the function could return the result obtained to save it in another variableand be able to continue working with this total price:

```
function calculates Total Price (price) {

var taxes = 1.16; var expenses Shipping = 10; var
Total price = (price * taxes) + expenses Shipping;

}
```

// The value returned by the function is stored in a variable var Total price =calculates Total Price (23.34);

// Continue working with the variable "Total price"

Fortunately, functions can not only receive variables and data but can also return the values they have calculated. To return values within a function,the reserved word return is used. Although functions can return values of any type, they can only return one value each time they are executed.

```
function calculates Total Price (price) {

var taxes = 1.16; var expenses Shipping = 10; var
Total price = (price * taxes) + expenses Shipping; return
total price;

} var Total price = calculates Total Price (23.34);
```

// Continue working with the variable "total price"

In order for the function to return a value, it is only necessary to write the reserved word return together with the name of the variable to be returned.In the previous example, the execution of the function arrives at the statement return total price; and at that time, it returns the value that contains the variable priceTotal.

As the function returns a value, at the point where the call is made, thename of a variable in which the returned value is stored must be indicated: var Total price = calculates Total Price (23.34);

If the name of any variable is not indicated, JavaScript does not show any errors and the value returned by the function is simply lost and thereforewill not be used in the rest of the program. In this case, it is also not mandatory that the name of the variable returned by the function matchesthe name of the variable in which that value is to be stored.

If the function reaches an instruction of type return, the indicated value is returned and the execution of the function ends. Therefore, all instructions that are included after a return are ignored and for that reason, the return statement is usually the last of most functions.

To make the above example more complete, another argument can be added to the function that indicates the percentage of taxes that must be added to the price of the product. Obviously, the new argument must be added to both the definition of the function and its call:

function calculates Total Price (price, percentage) {

Taxesvar expenses Shipping = 10; var price Taxes = (1 + percentage Taxes

/ 100) * price; var Total price = price with Taxes + expenses Shipping;return total price;

}

var Total price = calculates Total Price (23.34, 16); var other Total Price =calculates Total Price (15.20, 4);

To complete the previous exercise, the total price returned by the functioncan be rounded to two decimals:

function calculates Total Price (price, percentage) {

Taxesvar expenses Shipping = 10; var price Taxes = (1 + percentage Taxes

/ 100) * price; var Total price = price with Taxes + expenses Shipping;return priceTotal.toFixed (2);

} var Total price = calculates Total Price (23.34, 16);

Scope Of The Variables

The scope of a variable (called "scope" in English) is the area of the program in which the variable is defined. JavaScript defines two scopes for the variables: global and local.

The following example illustrates

the behavior of the scopes:function creates

Message () {

```
var message = "Test message";

} createMessage (); alert (message);
```

The previous example first defines a function called createMessage that creates a variable called message. Then, the function is executed by thecall createMessage (); and then, the value of a variable called message is shown by the alert () function.

However, when executing the above code, no message is displayed on the screen. The reason is that the message variable has been defined withinthe createMessage () function and is, therefore, a local variable that is only defined within the function.

Any instruction that is within the function can make use of that variable, but all instructions that are in other functions or outside of any function will not have the message variable defined. Thus, to display the message in the previous code, the alert () function must be called from within the createMessage ():

```
function function createMessage () {

var message = "Test message"; alert (message);

} createMessage ();
```

In addition to local variables, there is also the concept

of a global variable, which is defined at any point in the program (even within any function). var message = "Test message";

function sample Message () {alert (message);

}

The code above is the inverse example to the one shown above. Within the sample message function () you want to use a variable called message and that has not been defined within the function itself. However, if the previous code is executed, the message defined by the message variable is shown.

The reason is that in the previous JavaScript code, the message variablehas been defined outside of any function. These types of variables are automatically transformed into global variables and are available at any point in the program (even within any function).

Thus, although no variable called message has been defined inside the function, the previously created global variable allows the alert () instruction within the function to display the message correctly.

If a variable is declared outside of any function, it is automatically transformed into a global variable regardless of whether it is defined using the reserved word var or not. However, the variables defined within a function can be global or local.

If within a function, the variables are declared by

var are considered localand the variables that have not been declared by var, are automatically transformed into global variables.

Therefore, you can redo the code from the first example so that it displays the message correctly. To do this, simply define the variable within the function without the reserved word var, so that it becomes a global variable:

```
function createMessage () {
    message = "Test message";

}
createMessage (); alert (message);
```

What happens if a function defines a local variable with the same name asa global variable that already exists? In this case, the local variables prevail over the global ones, but only within the function:

```
var
```

```
message = "wins
the one outside";
function  sample
Message () {

        var message = "win the one inside"; alert (message);

        }

        alert (message); Sample Message (); alert (message);
```

The previous code shows the following messages on the screen:the outside one wins the inside one wins the outside one

Within the function, the local variable called message has more prioritythan the global variable of the same name, but only within the function.

What happens if a global variable is defined within a function with the same name as another global variable that already exists? In this other case, the global variable defined within the function simply modifies the value of the global variable defined above: variable

```
var  message = "wins  the  outside"; function
sample Message () {message = "win the inside"; alert
(message);

        }
```

alert (message); Sample
Message (); alert (message);In this
case, the messages shown are:

the one from outside wins the one from inside wins the
one from inside

The general recommendation is to define as local
variables all the variables that are exclusively used to perform
the tasks entrusted to each function. Global variables are
used to share variables between functions easily.

Break And Continue Statements

The control structure for is very simple to use, but it
has the disadvantage that the number of repetitions that can
be performed can only be controlled by the variables defined
in the loop update zone.

The break and continue statements allow you to
manipulate the normal behavior of the for loops to stop the
loop or to skip some repetitions.

Specifically, the break statement allows you to
abruptly terminate a loopand the continue statement allows
you to skip some repetitions of the loop.

The following example shows the use of the break
statement:

var string = "In a spot of the Stain whose name I
don't want to remember

..."; var letters = string.split (""); var result = "";for (i in letters) {

```
if (letters [i] == 'a') { break; } else { result + = letters
[i];

}}
```

alert (result); // shows "In a lug"

If the program reaches a break type instruction, it immediately exits theloop and continues executing the rest of the instructions outside the forloop. In the previous example, all the letters of a text string are traversed and when it encounters the first letter "a", the execution of the for loop is stopped.

The utility of break is to end the execution of the loop when a variable takesa certain value or when some condition is met.

Sometimes, what is desired is to skip some repetition of the loop when some conditions occur. Following the previous example, it is now desiredthat the output text remove all the letters "a" from the original text:

```
stringvar string = "In a spot of the Stain whose name
I don't want to remember ..."; var letters = string.split ("");
var result = "";

for (i in letters) {

if (letters [i] == 'a') { continue; } else { result + = letters
```

[i];

}} alert (result);

// shows "In a lugr of l Mnch whose name I don't want to cordr ..."

In this case, when a letter "a" is found, the loop is not terminated, but theinstructions of that repetition are not executed and Go directly to the next repetition of the for loop.

The utility of continue is that it allows you to use the for loop to filter the results based on some conditions or when the value of a variable matchesa certain value.

Other Control Structures

The flow control structures that have been seen (if, else, for) and the sentences that modify their behavior (break, continue) are not sufficient to perform some complex tasks and other types of repetitions. For this reason, JavaScript provides other flow control structures that are different and in some cases more efficient.

While Structure

The while structure allows you to create loops that run no more or more times, depending on the condition indicated. Its formal definition is:

while (condition) {...

}

The operation of the while loop is summarized in:

"While the indicated condition is fulfilled, repeat the instructions included within the loop indefinitely".

If the condition is not met even the first time, the loop is not executed. If the condition is met, the instructions are executed once and the condition is checked again. If the condition is still fulfilled, the loop is executed againand so it continues until the condition is not met.

Obviously, the variables that control the condition must be modified withinthe loop itself, since otherwise, the condition would always be met and the while loop would be repeated indefinitely.

Structure do ... while

The loop of type do ... while is very similar to the while loop, except that in this case the instructions of the loop are always executed at least the first time. Its formal definition is:

do {

} while (condition);

In this way, as the condition is checked after each repetition, the loopinstructions are always executed the first time. It is important not to forget that after the while () the character must be added; (contrary to whathappens with the simple while loop).

Using this loop you can easily calculate the factorial of a number:var result = 1; var number =

5;

```
do {
```

```
result * = number; // result = result * number
number--; } while (number> 0); alert (result);
```

In the previous code, the result is multiplied in each repetition by the valueof the variable number. In addition, in each repetition, the value of this variable number is decremented. The condition of the do ... while loop is that the number value is greater than 0 since the factorial of a number multiplies all numbers less than or equal to itself, but up to number 1 (the factorial of 5, for example, is 5 x 4 x 3 x 2 x 1 = 120).

As in each repetition, the value of the variable number is decremented and the condition is that number is greater than zero, in the repetition in which number is worth 0, the condition is no longer fulfilled and the programleaves the do loop ... while.

Switch Structure

The if ... else structure can be used to perform multiple checks and make complex decisions. However, if all conditions always depend on the same variable, the resulting JavaScript code is too redundant:

```
if (number == 5) {...} else if (number == 8) {...} else
if ( number == 20) {...
```

```
} else {...
```

```
}
```

In these cases, the switch structure is the most

efficient, since it is specially designed to easily handle multiple conditions on the same variable. Its formal definition may seem complex, although its use is very simple.

The switch structure is defined by the reserved keyword switch followed, in parentheses, by the name of the variable to be used in the comparisons. As usual, the instructions that are part of the switch are enclosed in quotes

{and}.

Within the switch, all the comparisons that you want to make on the valueof the variable are defined. Each comparison is indicated by the reserved word case followed by the value with which the comparison is made.

What happens if no value of the switch variable matches the values defined in the cases? In this case, the default value is used to indicate the instructions that are executed in the case where no case is met for the indicated variable.

Although default is optional, switch structures usually include it to define at least one default value for some variable or to display a message on the screen.

CHAPTER 4

DOM DOCUMENT OBJECT MODEL

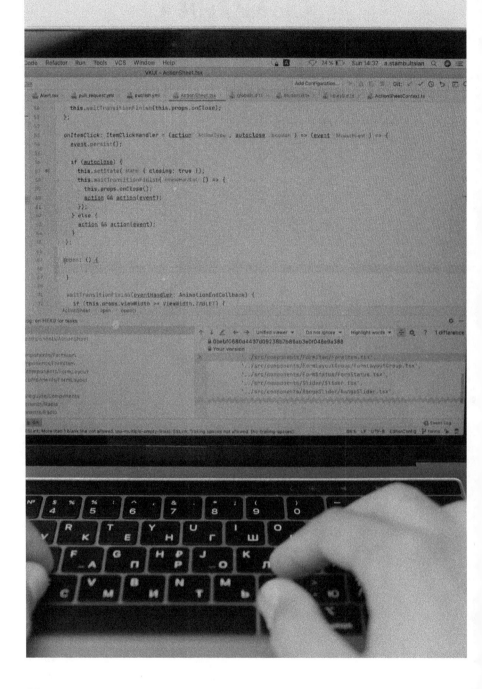

A big part of the development of dynamic web pages and complex web apps is the creation of the Document Object Model, or DOM. This is one of the most important things that has happened.

It lets web programmers work with XHTML pages as if they were XML documents. In fact, the DOM was originally designed to make it easy to manipulate XML documents.

Despite where it came from, the DOM is now a tool that can be used in most programming languages (Java, PHP, JavaScript), and the only difference is how it is implemented.

Node Tree

One of the usual tasks in programming web applications with JavaScript is the manipulation of web pages. In this way, it is usual to obtain the value stored by some elements (for example the elements of a form), create an element (paragraphs, <div>, etc.) dynamically and add it to the page, apply an animation to a item (to appear / disappear, to scroll, etc.).

All these usual tasks are very simple to perform thanks to DOM. However,in order to use the DOM utilities, it is necessary to "transform" the original page. A normal HTML page is nothing more than a succession of characters, so it is a very difficult format to manipulate. Therefore, web browsers automatically transform all web pages into a more efficient structure to manipulate.

This transformation is done by all browsers automatically and allows us to use the DOM tools very easily. The reason why the operation of this internal transformation is shown is that it determines the behavior of

DOM and therefore, the way in which pages are manipulated.

DOM transforms all XHTML documents into a set of elements called nodes, which are interconnected and that represent the contents of web pages and the relationships between them. Because of its appearance, the union of all nodes is called a "node tree".

It becomes the next tree of nodes. The root of the node tree of any XHTML page is always the same: a special type node called "Document".

From that root node, each XHTML tag is transformed into a node of type "Element". The conversion of tags into nodes is done hierarchically. In this way, only the HEAD and BODY nodes can derive from the root node. From this initial derivation, each XHTML tag is transformed into a node that derives from the node corresponding to its "parent tag".

The transformation of the usual XHTML tags generates two nodes: the firstis the "Element" type node (corresponding to the XHTML tag itself) and the second is a "Text" type node that contains the text enclosed by that XHTML tag.

Thus, the following XHTML tag:

<title> Simple page </title> Generates the following two nodes:

<p> This page is <strong> very simple </strong> </p> It generates thefollowing nodes:

' Type node "Element "corresponding to the <p> tag.

' Node of type "Text" with the textual content of the <p> tag.

' Since the content of <p> includes another XHTML tag inside it, the innertag is transformed into a node of type "Element" that represents the
    <strong> tag and derived from the previous node.

' The content of the <strong> tag generates another node of type "Text"that derives from the node generated by <strong>.

The automatic transformation of the page into a node tree always followsthe same rules:

' The XHTML tags are transformed into two nodes: the first is the tag itself and the second node is the son of the first and consists of the textualcontent of the label.

' If an XHTML tag is inside another one, the same procedure as above is followed, but the generated nodes will be child nodes of its parent tag.

As you can guess, the usual XHTML pages produce trees with thousandsof nodes. Even so, the transformation process is fast and automatic, being the functions provided by DOM (which will be seen later) the only ones that allow access to any node of the page easily and immediately.

Node Types

The full DOM specification defines 12 types of nodes, although the usual XHTML pages can be manipulated by handling only four or five types of nodes:

' Document, root node from which all other nodes in the tree derive.

' Element, represents each of the XHTML tags. It is the only node that cancontain attributes and the only one from which other nodes can derive.

' Attr, a node of this type is defined to represent each of the attributes of theXHTML tags, that is, one for each attribute = value pair.

' Text, node that contains the text enclosed by an XHTML tag.

' Comment, represents the comments included in the XHTML page.

The other types of existing nodes that are not to be considered are DocumentType, CDataSection, DocumentFragment, Entity, EntityReference, ProcessingInstruction, and Notation.

Direct Access To The Nodes

Once the complete DOM node tree is built automatically, it is now possibleto use the DOM functions to directly access any node in the tree. How to access a node in the tree is equivalent to accessing "a piece" of the page, once the tree is built, it is already possible to easily manipulate the page: access the value of an element, set the value of an element, move an element of the page, create and add new elements, etc.

DOM provides two alternative methods to access a specific node: access through its parent nodes and direct access.

The functions that DOM provides to access a node through its parent nodes consist of accessing the root node of the page and then its childnodes and the child nodes of those children and so on until the last node of the branch terminated by The searched node. However, when you want to access a specific node, it is much faster to directly access that node andnot reach the node through all its parent nodes.

For this reason, the functions necessary for hierarchical node access willnot be presented and only those that allow direct access to the nodes are shown.

Finally, it is important to remember that access to the nodes, their modification and their elimination are only possible when the DOM tree has been completely built, that is, after the XHTML page is fully loaded.

Normally the name attribute is unique to HTML elements that define it, so itis a very practical method to directly access the desired node. In the caseof HTML radiobutton elements, the name attribute is common to all radiobuttons that are related, so the function returns a collection of elements.

Internet Explorer 6.0 does not correctly implement this function, since itonly takes it into account for elements of type <input> and <img>. In addition, it also takes into consideration elements whose id attribute is equal to the function parameter.

getElementById ()

The getElementById () function is the most used

when developing dynamic web applications. This is the preferred function to directly access a nodeand be able to read or modify its properties.

The getElementById () function returns the XHTML element whose id attribute matches the parameter indicated in the function. Since the id attribute must be unique for each element of the same page, the function returns only the desired node. var header = document.getElementById ("header");

<div id = "header">

<a href="/" id="logo"> ... </a>

</div>

The getElementById () function is so important and so used in all webapplications, that almost all the examples and exercises that follow use it constantly.

Internet Explorer 6.0 also incorrectly interprets this function, since it also returns those elements whose name attribute matches the parameter provided to the function.

Creating And Deleting Nodes

Accessing the nodes and their properties (which will be seen later) is only part of the usual manipulations on the pages. The other usual operationsare to create and delete nodes from the DOM tree, that is, create and delete "chunks" from the web page.

Creating simple XHTML elements

As we have seen, a simple XHTML element, such as a paragraph, generates two nodes: the first node is of the Element type and representsthe <p> tag and the second node is of the Text type and represents the textual content of the <p> tag.

For this reason, creating and adding a new simple XHTML element to the page consists of four different steps:

1. Creation of an Element type node that represents the element.

2. Creation of a node of type Text that represents the content of theelement.

3. Add the Text node as the child node of the Element node.

4. Add the Element node to the page, in the form of a child node ofthe node corresponding to the place where you want to insert the element.

Thus, if you want to add a simple paragraph at the end of an XHTML page,it is necessary to include the following JavaScript code:

```
// Create node of type Element var paragraph = document.createElement("p");

// Create node of type Text var content = document.createTextNode ("HelloWorld!");

// Add the Text node as a child of the Element node parrafo.appendChild(content);
```

93

// Add the Element node as a child of the document.body.appendChild(paragraph) page;

The process of creating new nodes can become tedious since it involvesthe use of three DOM functions:

' createElement (tag): it creates a node of type Element that represents theXHTML element whose tag is passed as a parameter.

' createTextNode (content): Creates a node of type Text that stores thetextual content of the XHTML elements.

' parent node.appendChild (son node): add a node as a child of anothernode.

Deleting Nodes

Fortunately, removing a node from the DOM tree on the page is mucheasier than adding it. In this case, it is only necessary to use the removeChild () function:

var paragraph = document.getElementById ("provisional"); paragraph.parentNode.removeChild (paragraph);

<p id = "provisional"> ... </p>

The removeChild () function requires the node to be deleted as a parameter. In addition, this function must be invoked from the parent element of that node to be deleted. The safest and fastest way to accessthe parent node of an element is through the nodeHijo.parentNode property.

Thus, to remove a node from an XHTML page, the removeChild () functionis invoked from the parentNode value of the node to be deleted. When a node is deleted, all the child nodes it has, are automatically deleted, so it is not necessary to manually delete each child node.

Direct Access To XHTML Attributes

Once a node has been accessed, the next natural step is to access and/or modify its attributes and properties. Through DOM, it is possible to easily access all XHTML attributes and all CSS properties of any element of the page.

The XHTML attributes of the page elements are automatically transformed into properties of the nodes. To access its value, simply indicate the nameof the XHTML attribute behind the name of the node.

CHAPTER 5

EVENTS

```
length,c=!1)}a.memory
return n.each(argum
function(){return
(a){var b=[["resolve"
function(){return e.done
.fail(c.reject)
2].disable,b[2][2
function(a,b,c){return
fail(g.reject):-1;return
n.readyWait>0
"readystatechange",K)
addEventListener("DOMCon
setTimeout(f,50)}J(),n.ready
"div"),e.style.css
1)),c.removeChild
/^(?:\{[\w\W]*\})
data(a,b,c)}else
if(k&&j[k]&&(e
void 0!==d&&(g[n.camelCase
Case)):b in d?b=[b
"embed ":!0,"object
:function(a,b)
Case(d.slice(5))
removeData(this
function(){n.dequeue
_removeData(a,b
dequeue(this
```

So far, all of the applications and scripts that have been made have one thing in common: they run from the first instruction to the last one in order. For example, if, for, while can be used to change the flow of the script and repeat some parts of the script and skip others based on certain conditions.

People don't use these types of apps because they don't interact with them and can't respond to the things that happen while an application is running. They aren't very useful. The good news is that JavaScript-based web applications can use the event-based programming model.

In this type of programming, the scripts are only there to wait for the user to "do something" before they start (press a key, move the mouse, close the browser window). Next, the script responds to the user's action by processing the information and coming up with a result.

Events make it possible for people to send information to the programs that use them. JavaScript has a lot of events that make it possible for the user to interact with the web pages and apps on them. When you press a key, it's an event, just like when you move the mouse, click on a button, or resize the browser window.

JavaScript lets you set a function for each of the events. In this way, when any event happens, JavaScript runs its function. They are called "event handlers" in English and are often translated as "event handlers."

Event Models

Creating web pages and applications has always been much more complex than it should be due to incompatibilities between browsers. Although there are dozens of standards for the technologies used, browsers do not fully support them or even ignore them.

The main incompatibilities occur in the XHTML language, in the support of CSS stylesheets and, above all, in the implementation of JavaScript. Of allof them, the most important incompatibility occurs precisely in the browser's event model. Thus, there are up to three different models to handle events depending on the browser in which the application runs.

Basic Event Model

This simple event model was introduced for version 4 of the HTML standard and is considered part of the most basic level of DOM. Althoughits features are limited, it is the only model that is compatible in all browsers and therefore, the only one that allows you to create applications that work the same way in all browsers.

Standard Event Model

The most advanced versions of the DOM standard (DOM level 2) define a completely new and much more powerful event model than the original. All modern browsers include it, except Internet Explorer.

Internet Explorer Event Model

Internet Explorer uses its own event model, which is similar but incompatible with the standard model. It was first used in Internet Explorer4 and Microsoft decided to continue using it in the other versions, despitethe fact that the company had participated in the creation of the DOM standard that defines the standard event model.

Basic Event ModelTypes Of Events

In this model, each XHTML element or tag defines its own list of possible events that can be assigned. The same type of event (for example, clicking the left mouse button) can be defined for several different XHTML elements and the same XHTML element can have several different events associated.

The name of each event is constructed using the prefix on, followed by the English name of the action associated with the event. Thus, the event of clicking an element with the mouse is called onclick and the event associated with the action of moving the mouse is called onmousemove.

The most used events in traditional web applications are onload to wait for the page to load completely, the events onclick, onmouseover, onmouseout to control the mouse and onsubmit to control the submission of forms.

The typical actions that a user performs on a web page can lead to a succession of events. Pressing for example on a button of type <input type= "submit"> triggers the events onmousedown, onclick, onmouseup and onsubmit consecutively.

Event Handlers

A JavaScript event by itself lacks utility. For events to be useful, JavaScript functions or code must be associated with each event. In this way, when an event occurs, the indicated code is executed, so the application can respond to any event that occurs during its execution.

The functions or JavaScript code defined for each event are called "event handler" and since JavaScript is a very flexible language, there are several different ways to indicate the handlers:

- Handlers as attributes of the XHTML
- elements. Handlers as external JavaScript functions. "Semantic" handlers.

Event handlers as XHTML attributes

This is the simplest and least professional method of indicating the JavaScript code that should be executed when an event occurs. In thiscase, the code is included in an attribute of the XHTML element itself. In the following example, we want to show a message when the user clicks ona button:

```
<input type = "button" value = "Click me and you will see"
onclick = "alert ('Thanks for clicking');" />
```

In this method, XHTML attributes are defined with the same name as the events to be handled. The previous example only wants to control theevent of clicking with the mouse, whose name is onclick. Thus, the XHTML element for which you want to define this event must include an attribute called onclick.

The content of the attribute is a text string that

contains all the JavaScript instructions that are executed when the event occurs. In this case, theJavaScript code is very simple (alert ('Thanks for clicking');), since it is only about displaying a message.

In this other example, when the user clicks on the <div> element a message is displayed and when the user hovers the mouse over the element, another message is displayed:

<div onclick = "alert ('You clicked with the mouse'); " onmouseover = "alert('You just ran over the mouse');">

You can click on this element or just hover over the mouse

</div>

This other example includes one of the most used instructions in olderJavaScript applications :

<body onload = "alert ('The page has been fully loaded');"> ...

</body>

The previous message is displayed after the page has been fully loaded, that is after it has been loaded downloaded your HTML code, your images and any other object included in the page.

The onload event is one of the most used since, as seen in the DOMchapter, the functions that allow access and manipulation of the nodes ofthe DOM tree are only available when the page has been fully loaded.

Event handlers and 'this' Variable

JavaScript variable defines a special variable called this that is createdautomatically and used in some advanced programming techniques. In events, the variable this can be used to refer to the XHTML element that caused the event.

Event handlers as external functions

The definition of event handlers in XHTML attributes is the simplest butleast advisable method of dealing with events in JavaScript. The main drawback is that it is complicated in excess as soon as a few instructions are added, so it is only recommended for the simplest cases.

If complex applications are made, such as the validation of a form, it is advisable to group all the JavaScript code into an external function and call this function from the XHTML element.

Following the previous example that shows a message when clicking on a button:

```
<input type = "button" value = "Click me and you will see"
onclick = "alert ('Thanks for clicking');" />
```
Using external functions can be transformed into:

```
function sample Message () {alert ('Thanks
for clicking');

}
```

```
<input type = "button" value = "Click me and you
will see" onclick = "sample Message ()" />
```

This technique consists of extracting all JavaScript instructions and grouping them into an external function. Once the function is defined, the function name is included in the attribute of the XHTML element, to indicate that it is the function that is executed when the event occurs.

The function call is made in the usual way, indicating its name followed by the parentheses and optionally, including all the necessary arguments and parameters.

The main drawback of this method is that in the external functions it is not possible to continue using the variable this and therefore, it is necessary to pass this variable as a parameter to the function.

In the previous example, the external function is called with the parameter this, which within the function is called element. The complexity of theexample is mainly due to the way in which different browsers store thevalue of the borderColor property.

While Firefox stores (in case the four edges match in color) the black value, Internet Explorer stores it as black black black black and Opera stores its hexadecimal representation # 000000.

Semantic event handlers

The methods that have been seen to add event handlers (as XHTML attributes and as external functions) have a serious drawback: they "dirty"the XHTML code of the page.

As is known, one of the basic good practices in the design of web pagesand applications is the separation of content (XHTML) and its appearanceor presentation (CSS). Whenever possible, it is also recommended to separate the contents (XHTML) and its behavior or programming (JavaScript).

Mixing the JavaScript code with the XHTML elements only helps to complicate the source code of the page, make it difficult to modify and maintain the page and reduce the semantics of the final document produced.

Fortunately, there is an alternative method to define JavaScript event handlers. This technique is an evolution of the method of external functions, since it is based on using the DOM properties of XHTML elements to assign all external functions that act as event handlers. So, the following example:

```
<input id = "clickable" type = "button" value = "Click me and you will see" onclick = "alert ('Thanks for clicking');" />
```

It can be transformed into:

```
// External function
function sample Message () {
alert ('Thanks for clicking');

}
```

// Assign the external function to the document.getElementById ("clickable") element. Onclick = sample Message;

// XHTML element

<input id = "pinchable" type = "button" value = "Click and see" /> Thetechnique of semantic handlers consists of:

1. Assign a unique identifier to the XHTML element using the id attribute.

2. Create a JavaScript function responsible for handling the event.

3. Assign the external function to the corresponding event in the desired element.

The last step is the key to this technique. First, you get the element towhich you want to associate the external function: document.getElementById ("clickable");

Next, a property of the element with the same name as the event to be handled is used. In this case, the property is onclick: document.getElementById ("clickable"). Onclick = ...

Finally, the external function is assigned by its name without parentheses. The most important thing (and the most common cause of errors) is to indicate only the name of the function, that is, dispense with the parentheses when assigning the function: document.getElementById ("clickable"). Onclick = sample Message;

If the parentheses are added after the name of the function, the function is actually running and saving the value returned by the function in the element onclick property.

// Assign an external function to an event of a document.getElementById ("pinchable") element. Onclick = sample Message;

// Execute a function and save its result in a property of a document.getElementById ("pinchable") element. Onclick =sampleMessage ();

The great advantage of this method is that the resulting XHTML code isvery "clean" since it does not mix with the JavaScript code. In addition,within the assigned external functions, the variable this can be used to refer to the element that causes the event.

The only drawback of this method is that the page must be fully loaded before the DOM functions assigned by the handlers to the XHTML elements can be used. One of the easiest ways to ensure that certain codeis to be executed after the page is fully loaded is to use the onload event:

window.onload = function () {

document.getElementById ("clickable"). Onclick = sample Message ; }

The prior art uses the concept of anonymous functions, which is not goingto be studied, but which allows to create a compact and very simple code.To ensure

107

that a JavaScript code is to be executed after the page has been fully loaded, you only need to include those instructions between the {and} symbols:

```
window.onload = function () {...

}
```

In the following example, you add events to elements of type input = text ofa complex form:

```
function highlights () {

//      JavaScript      code}
window.onload = function () {

    var      form                              =
    document.getElementById
    ("form");    var
    fieldsInput =           form.getElementsByTagName
("input");

    for (var i = 0; i <fieldsInput.length; i ++) {

    if (fieldsInput [i] .type == "text") {fieldsInput [i]
.onclick = highlights;

    }

    }

    }
```

Obtaining Event Information (Event Object)

Normally, event handlers require additional information to process their tasks. If a function, for example, is responsible for processing the onclick event, you may need to know what position the mouse was at the time of clicking the button.

However, the most common case in which it is necessary to know additional information about the event is that of the events associated with the keyboard. Normally, it is very important to know the key that has been pressed, for example, to differentiate the normal keys from the special keys (ENTER, tab, Alt, Ctrl., Etc.).

JavaScript allows you to obtain information about the mouse and keyboard using a special object called event. Unfortunately, different browsers have very notable differences in the treatment of information about events.

The main difference lies in the way in which the event object is obtained. Internet Explorer considers that this object is part of the window object and the rest of browsers consider it as the only argument that the event handling functions have.

Although it is a behavior that is very strange at first, all modern browsers except Internet Explorer magically and automatically create an argumentthat is passed to the managing function, so it is not necessary to include itin the call to the managing function. Thus, to use this "magic argument", itis only necessary to assign it a name, as browsers automatically create it.

In summary, in Internet Explorer type browsers, the event object is obtained directly by: var event = window.event;

On the other hand, in the rest of browsers, the event object is obtained magically from the argument that the browser automatically creates:

```
function handlerEvents (theEvent) {
var event = theEvent;


}
```

If you want to program an application that works correctly in all browsers, itis necessary to obtain the event object correctly according to each browser.

The following code shows the correct way to obtain the event object in anybrowser:

```
function
handlerEvents
(elEvento) { var
event          =
elEvento       ||
window.event; }
```

Once the event object is obtained, all the information related to the eventcan be accessed, which depends on the type of event produced.

Information about the event

The type property indicates the type of event produced, which is usefulwhen the same function is used to handle several events: var type = event.type;

The type property returns the type of event produced, which is equal to the name of the event but without the prefix on.

Using this property, the previous example in which a section of contentswas highlighted when you hover the mouse over.

Information about keyboard events

Of all the events available in JavaScript, keyboard-related events are the most incompatible between different browsers and therefore, the most difficult to handle. First, there are many differences between browsers, keyboards, and user operating systems, mainly due to differences between languages.

In addition, there are three different events for the keystrokes (onkeyup, onkeypress, and onkeydown). Finally, there are two types of keys: normal keys (such as letters, numbers and normal symbols) and special keys (such as ENTER, Alt, Shift, etc.)

When a user presses a normal key, three events occur in a row and in this order: onkeydown, onkeypress and onkeyup. The onkeydown eventcorresponds to the fact of pressing a key and not releasing it; the onkeypress event is the key press itself and the onkeyup event refers to the release of a key that was pressed.

The easiest way to obtain information about the key that has been pressedis through the onkeypress event. The information provided by the onkeydown and onkeyup events can be considered as more technical since they return the internal code of each key and not the character thathas been pressed.

Below is a list with all the different properties of all keyboard events in bothInternet Explorer and other browsers:

Keydown event:

- Same behavior in all browsers:

- KeyCode property:
internal code of the key
- CharCode property: not defined

- Keypress event:

- Internet Explorer:

- keyCode property: the character code of the key that was pressedcharCode property: not defined

Other browsers:

- keyCode property: for normal keys, not defined. For special keys,the internal code of the key.

- charCode property: for normal keys, the character code of the keythat was pressed. For special keys, 0.

- Keyup event:

- Same behavior in all browsers:

- KeyCode property:
internal code of the key
- charCode property: not defined

To convert the code of a character (not to be confused with the internal code) when character representing the key that was pressed, the String.fromCharCode () function is used.

When you press the a key in the Firefox browser, the following sequence of events is displayed:

------- -------- -----

Event type: keydown KeyCode property: 65

charCode property: 0Character pressed:?

Event type: keypress KeyCode property: 0

charCode property: 97Character pressed: a

Event type: keyup KeyCodeproperty : 65

charCode property: 0 Character pressed:?

Pressing the A key (the same key, but having previously activated thecapital letters) shows the following sequence of events in the Firefox browser:

Event type: keydown KeyCodeproperty: 65

charCode property: 0 Character pressed:?

Event type: keypress KeyCode property: 0

charCode property: 65Character pressed: A

Event type: keyup KeyCodeproperty : 65

charCode property: 0 Character pressed:?

In the keydown and keyup events, the keyCode property is still valid in both cases. The reason is that keyCode stores the internal code of the key, so if the same key is pressed, the same code is obtained, regardless of the fact that the same key can produce different characters (for example, upper and lower case).

In the keypress event, the value of the charCode property varies, since character a is not the same as character A. In this case, the value ofcharCode matches the ASCII code of the pressed character.

Following the Firefox browser, if a special key is pressed, such as the tab, the following information is displayed:

----------------- ---------

Event type: keydown KeyCodeproperty: 9

charCode property: 0 Character pressed:?

---------------------- ---

Event type: keypress KeyCode property: 9

charCode property: 0Character pressed:?

Event type: keyup KeyCodeproperty: 9

charCode property: 0 Character pressed:?

The special keys do not have the charCode property, since only the internal code of the key pressed in the keyCode property is saved, in this case,code 9. If the Enter key is pressed, code 13 is obtained, the key the upper arrow produces code 38, etc. However, depending on the keyboard used to press the keys and depending on the arrangement of the keys dependingon the language of the keyboard, these codes may vary.

The result of the execution of the same example above in the InternetExplorer browser is shown below. Pressing the a key, the following information is obtained:

Event type: keydown KeyCodeproperty: 65

charCode property: undefined Character pressed:

Event type: keypress KeyCode property: 97

charCode property: undefined Character pressed:

Event type: keyup KeyCodeproperty: 65

charCode property: undefined Character pressed:

The keyCode property in the keypress event contains the ASCII code of the key character, so the character can be obtained directly using String.fromCharCode (keyCode).

If the A key is pressed, the information shown is identical to the previous one, except that the code that shows the keypress event changes to 65, which is the ASCII code of the A key:

------- ----------------

Event type: keydown KeyCodeproperty: 65

charCode property: undefined Character pressed:

------- ----------------

Event type: keypress KeyCode property: 65

charCode property: undefined Character pressed:

Event type: keyup KeyCodeproperty: 65

charCode property: undefined Character pressed :

When you press a special key like the tab, Internet Explorer displays thefollowing information:

-------------------- ---

Event type: keydown KeyCodeproperty: 9

charCode property: undefined Character pressed:

The codes shown for the special keys match those of Firefox and other browsers but remember that they may vary depending on the keyboard that is used and in the function of the arrangement of the keys for each language.

Finally, the altKey, ctrlKey and shiftKey properties store a Boolean valuethat indicates whether any of those keys were pressed when the keyboard event occurred. Surprisingly, these three properties work the same way in all browsers:

if (event.altKey) {

alert ('The ALT key was pressed'); }

Below is the case in which the Shift key is pressed and without releasing it, you press on the key that contains the number 2 (in this case, it refers tothe key that is at the top of the keyboard and by therefore, it does not referto the one found on the numeric keypad). Both Internet Explorer and Firefox show the same sequence of events:

- - - - - - - - - - - - - - - - - - - -

Event type: keydown KeyCodeproperty: 16

charCode property: 0 Character pressed:?

- - - - - - - - - - - - - - - - - - - -

Event type: keydown KeyCodeproperty: 50

charCode property: 0 Character pressed:?

- - - - - - - - - - - - - - - - - - - -

Event type: keypress KeyCode property: 0

charCode property: 34Character pressed: "

- - - - - - - - - - - - - - - - - - - -

Event type: keyup KeyCodeproperty : 50

charCode property: 0 Character pressed:?

- - - - - - - - - - - - - - - - - - - -

Type of event: keyup Property keyCode: 16

Property charCode: 0 Character pressed:?

The keypress event is the only one that allows to obtain the really pressed character, since when pressing on key 2 having previously pressed theShift key, the character is obtained ", which is precisely the one that shows the keypress event.

The following JavaScript code allows you to correctly obtain in any browser the character corresponding to the key pressed:

```
function handler (elEvento) {

var event = elEvento || window.event; var character = event.charCode || event.keyCode; alert ("The clicked character is:" + String.fromCharCode(character));

} document.onkeypress = handler;
```

Information about mouse events

The most relevant information about mouse-related events is the coordinates of the mouse pointer position. Although the origin of the coordinates is always in the upper left corner, the point taken as a reference of the coordinates may vary.

In this way, it is possible to obtain the position of the mouse with respect to the computer screen, with respect to the browser window and with respectto the HTML page itself (which is used when the user has scrolled over the page). The simplest coordinates are those that refer to the position of the pointer with respect to the browser window, which are obtained through the clientX and clientY properties:

function showsInformation (the Event) {

var event = the Event || window.event; var coordinateX = event.clientX; var coordinateY = event.clientY; alert ("You clicked on the position:" + coordinate X + "," + coordinate Y);

} document.onclick = sampleInformation;

The coordinates of the position of the mouse pointer with respect to the full screen of the user's computer are obtained in the same way, using the screenX and screenY properties:

var coordinateX = event.screenX; var coordinateY = event.screenY;

In many cases, it is necessary to obtain another pair of different coordinates: those corresponding to the position of the mouse with respectto the origin of the page. These coordinates do not always coincide with the coordinates regarding the origin of the browser window since the user can scroll over the web page. Internet Explorer does not provide these coordinates directly, while other browsers do. In this way, it is necessary to detect if the browser is Internet Explorer type and if so, perform a simple calculation.

The ie variable is true if the browser in which the

script is run is of type Internet Explorer (any version) and false otherwise. For the rest of thebrowsers, the coordinates regarding the origin of the page are obtainedusing the pageX and pageY properties. In the case of Internet Explorer, they are obtained by adding the position with respect to the browser window (clientX, clientY) and the page scrolling (document.body.scrollLeft, document.body.scrollTop).

CHAPTER 6

FORMS

JavaScript has always been used to make web forms in applications. This has always been one of the main jobs of JavaScript. In fact, one of the main reasons JavaScript was created was because it was needed to be able to check the form data right in the browser of the person who used it. People didn't have to start over when they made mistakes filling out forms this way.

However, the rise of AJAX applications has made the treatment of forms less important for JavaScript. Now, JavaScript is mostly used for asynchronous communication with servers and for changing applications on the fly, but it can also be used for many other things. Any JavaScript programmer will still need to know how to deal with forms.

Basic Properties Of Forms And Elements

JavaScript has numerous properties and functions that facilitate the programming of applications that handle forms. First, when a web page is loaded, the browser automatically creates an array called forms and that contains the reference to all forms on the page.

To access the forms array, the document object is used, so document.forms is the array that contains all the forms on the page. As it is an array, access to each form is done with the same syntax of the arrays. The following instruction accesses the first form of the page: document.forms [0];

In addition to the forms array, the browser automatically creates an array called elements for each of the forms on the page. Each array element contains the reference to all the elements (text boxes, buttons, drop-down lists, etc.) of that form. Using the syntax of the arrays, the following instruction obtains the first element of the first form of the page:document.forms [0] .elements [0];

Array syntax is not always so concise. The following example shows how to directly obtain the last element of the first form of the page: document.forms [0] .elements [document.forms [0] .elements.length-1];

Although this way of accessing the forms is quick and simple, it has a very serious inconvenience. What happens if the page layout changes and inthe HTML code the order of the original forms is changed or new forms are added? The problem is that "the first form of the page" could now beanother form different from what the application expects.

In an environment as changing as web design, it is very difficult to trust that the order of forms remains stable on a web page. For this reason, accessto forms on a page through the document.forms array should always be avoided.

One way to avoid the problems of the previous method is to access theforms of a page through its name (name attribute) or through its id attribute. The document object allows direct access to any form through its name attribute:

var formPrincipal = document.formulario; var Secondary form =document.otro_formulario;

```
<form name = "form"> ...

</form>

<form name = "other_form"> ...

</form>
```

Accessing the forms on the page in this way, the script works correctlyeven if the forms are reordered or new forms are added to the page. The elements of the forms can also be accessed directly through their name attribute:

var formPrincipal = document.form; var first Element = document.form.element;

```
<form name = "form">

<input type = "text" name = "element" />

</form>
```

Obviously, you can also access the forms and their elements using theDOM functions of direct access to the nodes. The following example uses the usual document.getElementById () function to directly access a formand one of its elements:

var formPrincipal = document.getElementById ("form"); var firstElement = document.getElementById ("element");

```
<form name = "form" id = "form">

<input type = "text" name = "element" id = "element" /> </form>
```

Regardless of the method used to obtain the reference to a form element, Each element has the following useful properties for application development:

- **type:** indicates the type of element being treated. For elements of type
  <input> (text, button, checkbox, etc.), it matches the value of its type attribute. For normal drop-down lists (<select> element) their value is select-one, which allows them to be differentiated from the lists that allow selecting

several elements at once and whose type is select-multiple. Finally, in elements of type <textarea>, the value of type is textarea.

- **form:** is a direct reference to the form to which the element belongs.Thus, to access the form of an element, you can use document.getElementById ("element_id"). Form

- **name:** get the value of the name attribute of XHTML. Only its value canbe read, so it cannot be modified.

- **value:** allows you to read and modify the value of the value attribute of XHTML. For the text fields (<input type = "text"> and <textarea>) get thetext that the user has written. For the buttons you get the text shown on the button. For the elements checkbox and radiobutton it is not very useful, as will be seen later.

Finally, the most used events in the handling of the forms are the following:

- **onclick:** event that occurs when you click with the mouse on an element. Normally it is used with any of the types of buttons that allow to define XHTML

(<input type = "button">, <input type = "submit">, <input type = "image">).

- **onchange:** event that occurs when the user changes the value of a text element (<input type = "text"> or <textarea>). It also occurs when the user selects an option from a drop-down list (<select>). However, the event only occurs if after making the change, the user moves to the next field of the form, which is technically known as "the other form field has lost focus."

- **onfocus:** event that occurs when the user selects an element of the form.

- **onblur:** complementary onfocus event, since it occurs when the user has deselected an element by selecting another element of the form. Technically, it is said that the previous element "has lost focus."

Basic Utilities For Forms Obtain the value of form fields

Most JavaScript techniques related to forms require reading and / or modifying the value of form fields. Therefore, below is how to get the valueof the most used form fields.

Text box and textarea

The value of the text displayed by these elements is obtained and setdirectly by the value property.

Radiobutton

When a group of radiobuttons is available, one generally does not want to obtain the value of the value attribute of any of them, but the importantthing is to know which of all the radiobuttons has been selected. The checked property returns true for the selected radiobutton and false in any other case.

Checkbox

Checkbox elements are very similar to radiobuttons, except that in thiscase, you should check each checkbox independently of the rest. The reason is that radiobutton groups are mutually exclusive and only one of them can be selected at a time. For their part, checkboxes can be selected independently from the others.

If the following checkboxes are available:

<input type = "checkbox" value = "conditions" name = "conditions" id ="conditions" /> I have read and accept the conditions

<input type = "checkbox" value = "privacy" name = "privacy" id = "privacy"

/> I have read the privacy policy

Using the checked property, it is possible to check if each checkbox hasbeen selected:

var element = document.getElementById ("conditions"); alert ("Element:" + element.value + "\ n Selected:" + element.checked);

element = document.getElementById ("privacy");

alert ("Element:" + element.value + "\ n Selected:" + element.checked);

Select

Drop-down lists (<select>) are the elements in which it is more difficult toobtain their value. If a drop-down list such as the following is available:

<select id = "options" name = "options">

```
<option value = "1"> First value </option>

<option value = "2"> Second value </ option>

<option value = "3"> Third value </option>

<option value = "4"> Fourth value </option>

</select>
```

In general, what is required is to obtain the value of the value attribute ofthe option (<option>) selected by the user. Obtaining this value is not easy, since a series of steps must be performed. In addition, to obtain the selected value, the following properties must be used:

' options, is an array created automatically by the browser for each drop- down list and containing the reference to all the options in that list. In this way, the first option in a list can be obtained through document.getElementById ("list_id"). Options [0].

' selectedIndex, when the user selects an option, the browser automatically updates the value of this property, which saves the index of the selected option. The index refers to the array options automatically created by the browser for each list.

```
// Get the reference to the list var list = document.getElementById("options");
```

```
// Get the index of the option selected var indexSelected = list.selectedIndex;
```

```
//  With the     index and     array
"options",  get     the   option selected     var
optionSelected = list.options [indexSelected];
```

```
// Get the value and the text of the selected option
varSelected text =optionSelected.text; var valueSelected =
optionSelected.value;
```

```
alert ("Selected option:" + selected text + "\ n Option
value:" + selected value);
```

As has been seen, to obtain the value of the value attribute correspondingto the option selected by the user, it is necessary to perform several steps. However, all necessary steps are usually abbreviated in a single instruction: var list = document.getElementById ("options");

```
// Get the value of the selected option var Value
Selected = list.options [list.selectedIndex] .value;
```

```
// Get the text that shows the selected option var
value Selected  = list.options [list.selectedIndex] .text;
```

The most important thing is not to confuse the value of the selectedIndex property with the value corresponding to the value property of the selected option. In the previous example, the first option has a value equal to 1. However, if this option is selected, the value of selectedIndex will be 0,since it is the first option of the array options (and the arrays start counting the elements in the number 0).

Set The Focus On An Element

In programming, when an element is selected and

you can write directly toit or you can modify any of its properties, it is said to have the focus of the program.

If a text box of a form has the focus, the user can write directly on it without having to previously click with the mouse inside the box. Likewise, if a drop- down list has the focus, the user can select an option directly by going up and down with the arrow keys.

By repeatedly pressing the TABULATOR key on a web page, the different elements (links, images, form fields, etc.) get the focus of the browser (the selected element each time usually shows a small dotted border).

If on a web page the form is the most important element, such as on asearch page or on a page with a form to register, it is considered a good usability practice to automatically assign the focus to the first element of the form when load the page

To assign the focus to an XHTML element, the focus () function is used.

Error Detection And Correction

JavaScript is an interpreted programming language, which means that most errors in the code cannot be detected until the scripts are executed. In this way, before considering a script as correct, it is necessary to test it in all the browsers on which it will be used.

When errors occur during the execution of a script, browsers provide some useful information to discover the exact point at which the error occurredand its possible solution. To solve the errors of a script is called "debug the script" or "debug the script" (term that comes from the English word "debug", which means "to eliminate the errors of an application").

Unfortunately, not all browsers provide the same useful information, which complicates the solution of errors for each type of browser. Below are the tools provided by each browser to detect and correct errors in JavaScript.

Error correction with Internet Explorer

Depending on your configuration, the Internet Explorer browser may have JavaScript error notification disabled. For this reason, it may first be necessary to activate warning messages about JavaScript errors. To activate notifications, access the Tools> Options menu, Advanced Options tab and activate the option.

Avoid sending a duplicate form

One of the usual problems with the use of web forms is the possibility of the user pressing twice in a row on the "Send" button. If the user's connectionis too slow or the response of the server is waiting, the original form is still displayed in the browser and for that reason, the user is tempted to click on the "Send" button again.

In most cases, the problem is not serious and it is even possible to controlit on the server, but it can be complicated in important application formssuch as those involving economic transactions.

For this reason, a good practice in designing web applications is usually to disable the send button after the first press. The following example shows the necessary code:

```
<form id = "form" action = "#"> ...
```

```
<input type = "button" value = "Send" onclick = "this.disabled = true; this.value = ' Sending ... '; this.form.submit () "/> </form>
```

When you click on the form submit button, the onclick event occurs on the button and therefore, the JavaScript instructions contained in the onclick attribute:

1. First, the button is disabled by the instruction this.disabled = true
    ;. This is the only instruction necessary if you only want to disable a button.

2. Next, the message shown by the button is changed. From the original "Send" is passed to the most appropriate "Sending ..."

3. Finally, the form is sent using the submit () function in the following instruction: this.form.submit ()

The button in the previous example is defined using a button of type <input type = "button" />, since the JavaScript code shown does not work correctly with a button of type <input type = "submit" />. If a submit type button is used, the button is disabled before submitting the form and therefore the form ends without being sent.

Limit the character size of a textarea

The most important lack of form fields of type textarea is the impossibility of limiting the maximum number of characters that can be entered, similar tothe maxlength attribute of normal text boxes.

JavaScript allows you to add this feature very easily. First of all, it should be remembered that with some events (such as onkeypress, onclick, and onsubmit), normal behavior can be avoided if false is returned.

Avoiding normal behavior is equivalent to completely modifying the usual behavior of the event. If for example the value false is returned in theonkeypress event, the key pressed by the user is not taken into account. If false is returned in the onclick event of an item as a link, the browser does not load the page indicated by the link.

If an event returns the value true, its behavior is the usual one:

<textarea onkeypress = "return true;"> </textarea>

In the textarea of the previous example, the user can type any character, since the onkeypress event returns true and therefore, its behavior is normal and the pressed key becomes a character within the textarea.

However, in the following example:

<textarea onkeypress = "return false;"> </textarea>

Since the value returned by the onkeypress event is equal to false, the browser does not execute the default behavior of the event, that is, the Pressed key is not transformed into any character within the textarea. No matter how many times the keys are pressed and the pressed key does not matter, that textarea will not allow you to type any character.

Taking advantage of this feature, it is easy to limit the number of characters that can be written in a textarea type element: it is checked if the maximum number of characters allowed has been reached and if so, the usual behavior of the event is avoided and therefore, additional characters arenot added to the textarea:

```
function limit (maximum Characters) {

var element = document.getElementById ("text"); if
(element.value.length> = maximum Characters) {

return false;

} else { return true;

}

}
```

```
<textarea id = "text" onkeypress = "return limits
(100);"> </textarea>
```

In the previous example, with each key pressed, the total number of characters in the textarea is compared with the maximum number of characters allowed. If the number of characters is equal to or greater thanthe limit, the value false is returned and therefore, the default behavior of onkeypress is avoided and the key is not added.

Restrict allowed characters in a text box

Sometimes, it may be useful to block certain specific characters in a textbox. If for example, a text box expects a number to be entered, it may be interesting not to allow the user to enter any character that is not numeric.

When a key is pressed, it is checked whether the character of that key is within the characters allowed for that <input> element.

If the character is within the allowed characters, true is returned and therefore the onkeypress behavior is usual and the key is written. If the character is not within the allowed characters, false is returned and

therefore normal onkeypress behavior is prevented and the key is not written to the input.

In addition, the previous script always allows the pressing of some special keys. In particular, the BackSpace and Delete keys to delete charactersand the Left Arrow and Right Arrow keys to move in the text box can always be pressed regardless of the type of characters allowed.

Validation

The main utility of JavaScript in the handling of forms is the validation of the data entered by users. Before sending a form to the server, it is recommended to validate the data inserted by the user through JavaScript.In this way, if the user has made an error when filling out the form, he can

137

be notified instantly, without waiting for the response from the server.

Reporting errors immediately through JavaScript improves user satisfaction with the application (what is technically known as "improving the user experience") and helps reduce the processing load on the server.

Normally, the validation of a form consists of calling a validation function when the user clicks on the form submit button. In this function, it is checked whether the values entered by the user meet the restrictions imposed by the application.

Although there are as many possible checks as different form elements, some checks are very common: that a mandatory field is filled in, that the value of a drop-down list is selected, that the indicated email address is correct, that the date entered is logical, that a number has been entered where required, etc.

Below is the basic JavaScript code needed to incorporate validation into a form:

<form action = "" method = "" id = "" name = "" onsubmit = "return validation ()"> ...

</ form >

And the validation function scheme () is as follows:

function validation () {if (condition that the first field of the form must meet)

```
{// If the condition is not met ... alert ('[ERROR]
The field must have a valueof ... '); return false;

}
```

else if (condition that the second field of the form must meet) {// If the condition is not met ... alert ('[ERROR] The field must have a value of ...'); return false;

```
} ... else if (condition that the last field of the form
```
must meet) {// If the condition is not met ... alert ('[ERROR] The field must have a value of ...'); return false;

```
}
```

// If the script has reached this point, all conditions // have been met, so thevalue true return true is returned;

```
}
```

The operation of this validation technique is based on the behavior of the JavaScript onsubmit event. Like other events such as onclick andonkeypress, the event onsubmit varies its behavior depending on the value that is returned.

Thus, if the onsubmit event returns true, the form is sent as it normallywould. However, if the onsubmit event returns the value false, the form isnot sent. The key to this technique is to check each and every element ofthe form. When an incorrect item is found, the value false is returned. If no error is found, the value true is returned.

Therefore, the onsubmit event of the form is defined first as: onsubmit = "return validation ()"

Since the JavaScript code returns the value resulting from the validation function (), the form will only be sent to the server if that function returnstrue In the event that the validation () function returns false, the form will remain unsent.

Within the validation function () all conditions imposed by the applicationare checked. When a condition is not met, false is returned and thereforethe form is not sent. If the end of the function is reached, all conditions have been met correctly, so true is returned and the form is sent.

The notification of mistakes made depends on the design of each application. In the code in the previous example, messages are simplyshown by the alert () function indicating the error produced. The best designed web applications show each error message next to the corresponding form element and also usually display a main message indicating that the form contains errors.

Once the scheme of the validation function () is defined, the corresponding code must be added to this function to all the checks carried out on the elements of the form. Below are some of the most common validations of form fields.

Validate a mandatory text field

This is to force the user to enter a value in a text box or text box in which itis mandatory.

For a mandatory text field to be completed, it is checked that the value entered is valid, that the number of characters entered is greater than zero, and that only blank spaces have not been entered.

The reserved word null is a special value that is used to indicate "no value".If the value of a variable is null, the variable does not contain any value of type object, array, numeric, text string or Boolean.

The second part of the condition requires that the text entered be longerthan zero characters, that is, that it is not an empty text.

Finally, the third part of the condition (/^\s+$/.test(value)) requires that the value entered by the user is not only made up of blanks. This verification is based on the use of "regular expressions", a common resource in any programming language but which due to its great complexity will not be studied. Therefore, it is only necessary to literally copy this condition, taking special care not to modify any character of the expression.

Validate a text field with numerical values

This involves forcing the user to enter a numerical value in a text box. TheJavaScript condition consists of:

value = document.getElementById ("field"). Value; if (isNaN (value)) {return false;

}

If the content of the value variable is not a valid number, the condition is not met. The advantage of using the internal isNaN () function is that it simplifies checks, since

JavaScript takes care of taking into account decimals, signs, etc.

Validate an email address

This is to force the user to enter an email address with a valid format. Whatis checked is that the address seems valid, since it is not checked if it is a real and operational email account. The JavaScript condition consists of:

value = document.getElementById ("field"). Value; if (! (/ \ w {1,} [@] [\ w \ -]

{1,} ([.] ([\ w \ -]
{1,})) {1,3} $ /. test (value)))
{return false;

}

The check is done again using regular expressions since the valid email addresses can be very different. Although the condition is very complex, if it is copied literally, it can be applied to any case in which you need to checkan email address.

Validate a date

Dates are usually the most complicated form fields to validate for the multitude of different ways in which they can be entered. The followingcode assumes that in some way the year, month and day entered by theuser have been obtained:

142

```
var year = document.getElementById ("year"). Value;
var month = document.getElementById ("month"). value;
var dia = document.getElementById ("dia"). value; value =
new Date (year, month, day);

if (! isNaN (value)) { return false;

}
```

The Date function (year, month, day) is an internal JavaScript function that allows you to build dates from the year, month and day of the date. It isvery important to keep in mind that the month number is indicated from 0 to 11, with 0 being the month of January and 11 the month of December. The days of the month follow a different numbering since the minimum allowed is 1 and the maximum 31.

The validation consists of trying to construct a date with the data providedby the user. If the user data is not correct, the date cannot be constructed correctly and therefore the form validation will not be correct.

Validate a DNI number

This is to verify that the number provided by the user corresponds to a valid National Identity Document or DNI number. Although for each country or region the requirements of the identity document of the people may vary, a generic example easily adaptable is shown below. The validation must not only verify that the number consists of eight digits and one letter, but it isalso necessary to verify that the indicated letter is correct for the entered number:

```
value = document.getElementById ("field"). Value;
var letters = ['T', 'R', 'W', 'A', 'G', 'M', 'Y', 'F', 'P', 'D', 'X', 'B ',' N ',' J ',

'Z ',' S ',' Q ',' V ',' H ',' L ',' C ',' K ',' E ',' T '] ;

if (! (/ ^ \ d {8} [AZ] $ /. test (value))) {return false;

}

if (value.charAt (8)! = letters [(value.substring (0, 8))% 23]) {return false;

}
```

The first check ensures that the format of the number entered is correct, that is, that it consists of 8 consecutive numbers and one letter. If the letter is at the beginning of the numbers, the check would be / ^ [AZ] \ d {8} $ /. If instead of eight numbers and one letter, ten numbers and two letters are required, the check would be / ^ \ d {10} [AZ] {2} $ / and so on.

The second check applies the algorithm for calculating the letter of the DNI and compares it with the letter provided by the user. The algorithm of each identification document is different, so this part of the validation must be adapted accordingly.

Validate a telephone number

Telephone numbers can be indicated in very different

ways: with a national prefix, with an international prefix, grouped in pairs, separating numberswith dashes, etc.

The following script considers that a telephone number consists of nine consecutive digits and without spaces or dashes between the figures:

```
value = document.getElementById ("field"). Value; if (! (/ ^ \ d {9} $ /. test (value))) {

return false;

}
```

Again, the JavaScript condition is based on the use of regular expressions, which check if the indicated value is a succession of nine consecutivenumbers.

Validate that a checkbox has been selected

If an element of type checkbox is mandatory, JavaScript allows you tocheck it very easily:

```
element = document.getElementById ("field"); if (! element.checked) {return false;

}
```

Validate that a radiobutton has been selected

Although it is a case similar to that of the checkboxes, the validation of the radiobuttons presents an important difference: in general, the verificationthat is made is that the user has selected some radiobutton from those that form a certain group Using JavaScript, it is easy to determine if a

145

radiobutton has been selected from a group.

Clocks, Counters And Time Intervals

Sometimes, some web pages display a clock with the current time. If the clock must be updated every second, the time cannot be displayed directly on the HTML page generated by the server. In this case, although there are alternatives made with Java and Flash, the easiest way to do this is toshow the time of the user's computer using JavaScript.

To create and display a clock with JavaScript, you must use the internalDate () object to create dates/times and the utilities that allow you to define counters, to update the clock every second.

The Date () object is a utility that provides JavaScript to create dates and times. Once a date type object has been created, it can be manipulated to obtain information or perform calculations with dates. To obtain the current date and time, it is only necessary to create a Date () object without passing any parameters: var dateTime = new Date ();

Using the code above, you can build a very basic clock that does notupdate its content:

var dateHour = new Date (); document.getElementById ("clock"). innerHTML = dateTime;

<div id = "clock" />

When the page is loaded, the previous example would show a text similarto the following in the <div> reserved for the clock:

Thu Aug 02 2007 19:35:19 GMT + 0200 (Summer time romance)

This first built clock has many differences from the clock you want to build. First, it shows much more information than is necessary. In addition, itsvalue is not updated every second, so it is not a very practical clock.

The Date () object provides very useful functions for obtaining information about the date and time. Specifically, there are functions that directly obtain the hour, minutes and seconds.

Using the getHours (), getMinutes () and getSeconds () functions of theDate object, the clock can only display time information. The result of the previous example would be a clock like the following:

20: 9: 21

If the hour, minute or second is less than 10, JavaScript does not add 0 ahead, so the result is not entirely satisfactory.

To complete the clock, you just need to update its value every second. To achieve this, you must use special JavaScript functions that allow you to execute certain instructions when a certain period of time has elapsed.

The setTimeout () function allows you to execute a

function after a specified period of time has elapsed. The definition of the function is: setTimeout (functionName, milliseconds);

The function to be executed must be indicated by its name without parentheses and the time that must elapse until it is executed is indicatedin milliseconds. In this way, if a function is created to show the time of the clock and it is called Sample Clock (), it can be indicated that it is executed within 1 second.

However, the code simply shows the contents of the clock 1 second afterthe page loads, so it is not very useful. To execute a function periodically, you use a JavaScript function very similar to setTimeout () that is called setInterval (). Its definition is: setInterval (functionName, milliseconds);

The definition of this function is identical to the setTimeout () function, except that in this case, the programmed function is executed infinitelyperiodically with a period of time between executions of as many milliseconds as they have been established.

Thus, to build the complete clock, a periodic execution of the sample function Clock () is established every second.

Using the Date object and its functions, it is possible to build "countdown", that is, clocks that show the time left until an event occurs. In addition, the setTimeout () and setInterval () functions can be very useful in other programming techniques.

CONCLUSION

Thank you for making it to the end of Javascript For Beginners. Let's hope it was useful and gave you all the tools you need to reach your goals, no matter what they are.

The goal of this book was to help people learn Java programming and to make sure that everyone can use this language to its fullest. This book is meant to help people learn more about Javascript and make sure there isn't a lot of confusion about it. Finally, here's a little history on Javascript.

In order to "standardize a cross-platform scripting language that is not owned by any one company," the European Computer Manufacturers Association (ECMA) set up the TC39 committee. As part of the TC39 committee, the ECMA-262 standard was the first one to be written by them. In this standard, for the first time, the ECMAScript language is defined.

For this reason, some programmers prefer to use the ECMAScript name for the JavaScript language. A lot of people don't know this, but JavaScript is nothing more than Netscape's version of ECMAscript.

ECMA-262 is a standard that was adopted by the ISO through its IEC commission. This standard is called ISO / IEC- 16262.

ECMA has written a lot of standards about ECMAScript.

The fourth version of ECMA-262 is being worked on, and it could include things like packages, namespaces, explicit class definitions, and more.

There are also other standards that are related to ECMAScript, such as the ECMA-357 standard. This standard defines an extension called E4X that allows JavaScript and XML to be mixed together.

A good review on Amazon is always welcome if you found this book useful in any way.

CPSIA information can be obtained
at www.ICGtesting.com
Printed in the USA
BVHW050544140223
658474BV00023B/358